For Justice
and Enduring Peace

FOR JUSTICE AND ENDURING PEACE

One Hundred Years of Social Witness

Jessica M. Smith

Epilogue by The Rev. Dr. Susan T. Henry-Crowe

Abingdon Press
Nashville

FOR JUSTICE AND ENDURING PEACE:
ONE HUNDRED YEARS OF SOCIAL WITNESS

Copyright © 2023 by Abingdon Press

ISBN: 978-1-7910-3128-2

Library of Congress Control Number: 2023941538

MANUFACTURED IN THE UNITED STATES OF AMERICA

Contents

Preface

This anthology is a tribute to the many Methodists who have carried the Wesleyan tradition of social witness forward over the past one hundred years. It recalls the concerns and witness of social movements as interpreted through the lens of the General Board of Church and Society (also known as "Church and Society") and its predecessor bodies.

Since 1923, the United Methodist Building (UMB) has stood on Capitol Hill in Washington, D.C and provided a public witness for peace and justice.[1] For decades, it has offered hospitality for Methodists, other faith leaders, and people of good conscience across the United States and the world. The General Board of Church and Society remains its proprietor. In addition to its presence on Capitol Hill, the agency's ministries also include engaging member states of the United Nations (UN) on issues of international affairs and peace at the Church Center for the United Nations (CCUN) in New York City.

The publication of this anthology is not the first time that Church and Society has taken a retrospective look at the building and agency's legacy. The first general secretary Clarence True Wilson and former staff Herman Will, Astor Kirk, and John P. Adams wrote and published works related to their ministries. In 1998, during the 50th anniversary of the UN Declaration of Human Rights, Church and Society published an entire issue in its magazine *Christian Social Action* (CSA) on Methodism and human

---

1. The building was originally named the Methodist Building upon its construction. However, when the editor is referring to the building, the text will reflect its current name of the United Methodist Building (UMB).

rights. For the UMB's 75th anniversary in 1999, the CSA magazine published articles telling the story of the building and agency's history. This text seeks to honor the legacies of previous publications and extend their contributions to the current era.

The articles in this volume highlight how many of the issues Church and Society engages today reflect and promote the same basic principles that Methodists stood for decades ago. Racism, criminal justice, police brutality, migrant justice, immigration, non-violence, peace, public health, economic justice, creation care, and environmental racism are topics that previous generations have wrestled with and articulated as important issues. More significantly, their positions on these issues often speak to a vision that carries forward today—that all people are created by God as equal and deserve equal rights; economic policy must include accounting for environmental justice; welcoming of others and radical hospitality are basic Christian responsibilities; non-violence and peace in international conflict are imperative; and seeking liberation with the poor, the imprisoned, and those who have been robbed of their basic rights and lands are all essential parts of the Methodist social witness.

The articles presented here were selected and are republished from original newsletters and magazines of Church and Society and its predecessor bodies. With such a large repository of material, particular criteria for inclusion had to be employed for the purposes of this anthology. The selection process entailed curating articles that would accomplish an array of things both individually and collectively. Like the instruments in an orchestra, each piece needed to be able to both sing on its own and complement neighboring selections when read together. Therefore, some criteria was employed to select the articles enclosed.

First, it was necessary to determine the denominational perspective of this work. Scholars from various universities, ecumenical and interfaith partners, and other entities authored articles on issues. While all quite compelling, this volume features the voices of *Methodist* leaders who championed social issues in collaboration with Church and Society and its predecessor bodies. From future bishops to agency directors to local church pastors to organizers, each voice featured in this work speaks to the legacy and contributions of Methodist leaders seeking God's justice and peace. Every attempt was made to republish the original text. Minor typos were edited for clarity.

Second, the articles were chosen and arranged for optimal relevance and approachability for today's reader. To achieve this goal, the anthology focuses on observational essays about historic events, first person narratives, and public statements that illuminate an issue or event in an accessible way. The articles are arranged chronologically under four major issue areas. The four major sections include Health and Wholeness; Civil and Human Rights; Peace; and Economy and Ecology. Each major section attempts to give an overview of major topics, including what was unable to be represented in the volume.

Like any compilation, there are some excellent pieces in the archival materials including, for example, U.S. federal policy, global affairs, Bible studies, poetry, liturgical resources, and summaries of major events in the life of the church. However, they were either too esoteric for the current reader or merit their own study outside the purview of this one.

As noted previously, it is remarkable to see the ways that the principles for Methodist social witness have remained clear for many decades. At the same time, many articles include language that might have been culturally acceptable or common at the time of their writing but are today known to include offensive, pejorative, or exclusionary language. We lament the fact that racist, gendered, and colonialist language and perspectives continue to do harm against historically marginalized communities, particularly communities of color. We invite readers to read these texts critically and examine the ways that language can reflect and reinforce structural injustices. We cannot look away at this history, while at the same time we cannot condone such language or attitudes as an acceptable part of our shared lives today.

Third, this volume also demonstrates how the voices of authority on issues has changed. While early articles were almost exclusively authored by white men, we see that those who speak on an issue shift over time. Authorship grew more inclusive, increasingly shifting away from a white perspective. Over time, the reflections begin to bring to the center the voices and communities that are directly impacted by an issue. Articles increasingly discuss finding solidarity among and across marginalized communities globally, rather than centering white, U.S. perspectives. While progress on the issue itself may seem slow or even barely recognizable, we can see how the board(s) increasingly sought to address the issues from the perspective of those most impacted by them. This is not to be seen as a completed effort or a final victory by any means. But it is something for which Methodists might honor and continue to seek.

Finally, these articles reflect the ways that the board(s) related to the larger Methodist connection and faith-based advocacy. Many of our efforts are not done in isolation but rather in partnership with other agencies as well as the Council of Bishops. Much of Church and Society and its predecessor body's ministry reflect the concerns of the General Conference. The 1980 General Conference's efforts to address President Carter and the Ayatollah on the Iran hostage crisis, for example, was supported by the board(s) through offering briefings and consultation as the General Conference responded to the crisis. Similarly, coalitions made up of secular, ecumenical, and inter-faith partners have been a central part of the board(s) advocacy efforts throughout the decades. From embarking on an inter-racial solidarity journey to Europe in the 1930's, to breaking ground on the CCUN in the 1950's, to supporting the Poor People's Campaign of 1968, to fighting for healthcare for all as early as the 1970's, Methodists have been consistently committed to working with diverse partners for God's justice and peace.

Our witness today stands on the shoulders of countless faith leaders who worked for the rights and dignity of God's creation and God's people. The Methodist witness for justice is one that has long come before this moment. The voices included in this volume are a tribute to all of those who, however imperfectly, however haltingly, sought after God's hope, righteousness, and love in the world. They spoke out, they marched, they advocated, they testified, they organized, they prayed, they mourned, they celebrated day by day for God's people and creation.

I would especially like to thank all of those who have contributed to the development of this work. Fitting of the tradition, this publication would not have been possible without the support of our sister agencies. Thanks to the General Board of Archives and History's support, particularly archivist Frances Lyons. Her hospitality and professionalism were so welcome in the discovery of early articles from the board(s). The editorial team of the General Board of Higher Education and Ministry, particularly John Clark and its publishing arm, allowed this work to move forward with the flexibility and support that was needed for its completion. Finally thanks to the General Board of Church and Society staff, including Aimee Hong, John Hill, Mark Harrison and Michelle Beadle. Thanks to the staff at the United Methodist Publishing House for their encouragement, patience, and support in publishing this project. Thanks to Greg McCollum for his editorial support and for the many, many months of transcribing over 100 articles, of which only a fraction are seen here. And of course, many thanks to Rev. Dr. Susan T. Henry-Crowe for her vision and leadership to see this work to its fruition.

Beginning of Construction of the New Methodist Building at 110 Maryland Ave NE, November 1922. Left to right: CH Mooers; Dr. R.J. Wade, Corresponding Secretary, Committee on Conservation and Advance; Eugene Phelps; Miss Ina I. Bates, Office Secretary; Miss Katherine Hansen; Miss Naomi Phelps; Miss Norma Gambin; R.V. Johnson, Field Secretary; Miss Anna M. Tilton; E.A. Grant; D. Stewart Patterson, Assistant Research Secretary; John Whitney, Board of Temperance, Prohibition, and Public Morals of the Methodist Episcopal Church. CHS 07083. General Photograph, DC Collection, DC History Center, Washington, D.C.

Board Members and Visitors to the Annual Meeting of the Board of Temperance, ca. 1920s. GBCS Photo.

JOHN NELSON CLARK COGGIN

Clarence True Wilson with Others at the Building Site with Cornerstone. Image from Clarence T. Wilson Collection, General Commission on Archives and History, Drew University, Madison, N.J. Image courtesy of the General Commission on Archives and History of The United Methodist Church, Madison, N.J.

Rev. Dr. John Nelson Clark Coggin, Staff Member, Board of Temperance, Prohibition, and Public Morals. From History of the American Negro and His Institutions: Washington D.C. Edition, Atlanta: A.B. Caldwell Publishing, 1922. Public Domain.

H34010 Methodist Building. Board of Temperance and Public Morals. Washington, D.C.

Methodist Building, Board of Temperance and Public Morals, Washington, D.C. From Cities 15-H34010, Clarence True Wilson Collection, General Commission on Archives and History. Image courtesy of the General Commission on Archives and History of The United Methodist Church, Madison, N.J.

Deets Pickett, Methodist Board of Temperance Research Secretary, 1920s. From GBCS Holdings. Photo by Reni Photos.

v Simpson Memorial Chapel, View from the Altar, 1951. From GBCS Holdings. Photo by Reni Photos.

Poster Developed by the Board of Temperance Concerning Regulation of Drinking and Driving. GBCS Photo.

Blakeslee-Lane, Baltimore—Washington Photographic Illustrators, Nation 6700, 911 G. St. N.W., Washington, D.C. From UM Building Holdings.

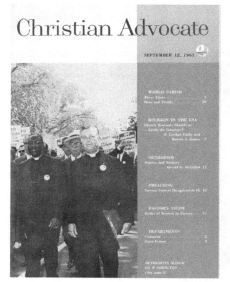

Methodists March on Washington, 1963. Photo by Ken Jones, The Christian Advocate, United Methodist Publishing House. Image courtesy of the General Commission on Archives and History of The United Methodist Church, Madison, N.J.

Dayton Edmonds, Native American Storyteller/ Musician at St. Louis National Training Event, 1987. GBCS Photo.

Summer Institute on Climate Change, Philippines, 2014. GBCS Photo.

GBCS Staff Member Rev. Cynthia Abrams Speaks at an Inter-Faith Rally at the U.S. Supreme Court in Favor of the Affordable Care Act, 2015. GBCS Photo.

EYA Summer Interns, Class of 2016. EYA Summer Interns, Class of 2016.

UM Building Green Roof Looking Toward U.S. Capitol. Installed 2013. Photo 2018. Photo by GBCS Staff.

Introduction

Like a flowing river with tributaries sourcing its waters, the General Board of Church and Society (or "Church and Society") can trace its formation, mission, and witness from many theological, ecclesial, social, and political streams. For the purposes of orienting the reader, we can consider particularly the following: (1) the formation and contributions of earlier denominational social witness bodies, (2) the Social Creed tradition and development of the Social Principles, (3) the construction of the United Methodist Building (UMB) in Washington, D.C., and ministries in the New York based office at the Church Center of the United Nations (CCUN).

First, the formal beginnings of the General Board of Church and Society can be traced to the 1968 General Conference in Dallas, Texas. The General Conference body was determining and ratifying the Plan of Union between the Evangelical United Brethren (EUB) Church and the Methodist Episcopal Church (MEC) for the purposes of creating the United Methodist Church (UMC). It was a remarkable moment in the life of the Methodist movement, and there were a great many dimensions to the union that had demanded negotiation between the MEC and the EUB.

Culturally, the country was in shock over the assassination of Martin Luther King Jr. only a month prior to the Dallas, Texas gathering. Racial segregation had plagued the MEC with its construction of the Central Jurisdiction, a system of racially segregating conferences across the denomination. The MEC had been studying the issue of racial segregation in the church since the 1950's and had been working toward eliminating the racially segregated Central Jurisdiction from its structure. The merger of 1968 furthered the work to eliminate the Central Jurisdiction and by 1972 the remaining segregated conferences had merged so that the formal structure of racial segregation in the UMC was eliminated. In addition to addressing the racist structure of the church, the UMC had to create its polity structure. Both the EUB and the ME Church held strong social witness commitments that were addressed through denominational agencies. The EUB's Commission on Christian Social Action was attuned to the concerns of society and church life but was hampered by capacity. The MEC had created the Board of Christian Social Concerns (CSC) in 1960 after merging three boards—the Board of World Peace, the Board of Social and Economic Relations, and the Board of Temperance. The UMC once again consolidated these entities to form the General Board of Church and Society, headquartered at the UMB in Washington, D.C.

Second, the Social Creed tradition contributed to how the church organized its social witness. Today, the Social Principles guide Church and Society's participation in social witness, providing the grounding for the legislative advocacy and educational work. Besides serving as a teaching document for the church as a whole, the Social Principles are a vital reference point for Church and Society to articulate Methodist values and positions. Its creation and development between 1968 and1972 set the foundation for social witness today.

Finally, expressions of Methodist social witness at Church and Society are anchored by the UMB in Washington, D.C., as well as the United Nations ministries in New York. Situated on Capitol Hill, the UMB stands as a site of hospitality for people of faith and good conscience who seek social justice. This landmark stands as witness to major events both triumphant and tragic in the nation and the world's history. The agency's United Nations Office in New York also reflects the vital contribution Methodist leaders have offered to the pursuit of world peace.

The General Board of Church and Society and Its Predecessor Bodies

The General Board of Church and Society's life and witness is intimately related to the mission and focus of previous bodies, particularly the three noted above—the Board of Temperance, the Board of World Peace, and the Board of Social and Economic Relations. Each held specific histories, geographic centers, and social programs; each of their histories informs the work and mission of the current board.

Board of Temperance, Prohibition and Public Morals

The Board of Temperance outlined above was the successor of the Board of Temperance, Prohibition, and Public Morals. The board was critical for both the construction of the UMB and the legacy of Methodism's commitment to a healthy society. The legacy of this board includes Church and Society's work on addressing gambling, alcohol, and other drugs, as well as public safety initiatives.

The Board of Temperance, Prohibition and Public Morals was authorized out of the Temperance Society by the 1916 MEC General Conference. Dr. Clarence True Wilson served as its Executive Secretary. Its headquarters were first in Chicago and then Topeka, Kansas, before coming to Washington, D.C.

Dr. Clarence True Wilson was a fiery and nationally recognized public promoter of prohibition. He spearheaded a vision for a nation that soberly pursued Christian moral action in the world. At a 1930 report to the board of directors published in the agency's magazine *The Voice*, Dr. Wilson outlined the meaning of the three aspects of the agency's name. Temperance referred to the educational services provided to encourage Methodists to abstain from "all habit-forming, irritant, narcotic drugs, including alcohol."[1] The board encouraged all Methodists to sign a pledge abstaining from addicting substances including liquor, narcotics, and opiates. The Board's Prohibition work addressed the health of the society by urging congressional passage of bills prohibiting the traffic of liquor. As Wilson writes, these laws against the

---

1. "Twentieth Annual Report of Clarence True Wilson," *The Voice*, January 1930.

selling of liquor helped to not only address the personal practice of abstention—as the temperance movement had done—but also to address "the conditions that make" persons dependent on habit-forming drugs.[2] The Board saw both the passage of the 18th Amendment and its repeal. Up through the 1950's, the Board continued its mission for a sober, healthy society advocating for laws related to curbing drunk driving and alcohol regulations on airplanes. Finally, as Wilson reports, the Public Morals program was instituted in 1916. The board was especially concerned with society's standards in film and theatre settings, the formation of young people, and prizefighting. Wilson relayed a close relationship between what he called its "two most dreaded scourges,—rum and war; within the nations, no rum; between the nations, no war."[3] For him, the Board's concern with public morality was directly related to its understanding of the effects of war: "We are in the aftermath of World War. One of the terrible things about war is its utter slump in public morals. All wars have the same effect. They break up home life, church ties, community standards, take men from family restraints and put them in abnormal conditions where they are in proximity to unrestrained evil."[4] As an antidote, the board encouraged Methodists "to register, to vote, to work, to pray"[5] as civic leaders fighting for the country's ideals.

The current board's program advocating for healthy families and communities as well as civic engagement is part of the legacy of this earlier board.

Board of World Peace

The Board of World Peace began as a Commission formed by the MEC in 1924. Its impetus was in large part spurred on by men returning from the war in Europe, and in the 1930's, the board conducted seminars across the country on the church and world peace. By 1940, the Commission's headquarters were established in Chicago with the following purpose: "to advance the interests of the Kingdom of our Lord through

---

2. Ibid., 2.

3. Ibid.

4. Ibid.

5. Ibid.

international justice and the spirit of good will throughout the world; to endeavor to create the will to peace, the conditions for peace, and the organization for peace; and to organize effective action in the Church for the advancement of peace."[6]

Many of the Board of World Peace leaders, including Charles F. Boss Jr. and Herman Will, were part of the national efforts to study and explore principles for a just, durable peace. In 1941, the Commission hosted a conference of the Federal Council of Churches at the Chicago Temple. Rev. Charles F. Boss Jr. was the secretary of the conference, and the Commission on World Peace published the conference's findings. These discussions contributed to the development and writing of the UN Charter of 1945.

In the 1950's, the Commission on World Peace published a remarkable newsletter, *The Methodist Peace Courier*, in which perspectives on nuclear disarmament, conscientious objection, stewardship, and trade policies were all discussed. By 1952, the Commission had been made a Board of World Peace and retained membership in the International Justice and Goodwill of the National Council of Churches, and through its executive secretary held a "cooperative relationship with the Church's Commission on International Affairs of the World Council of Churches." The board's head also was a liaison to the U.S. Department of State as well as the UN.[7]

Today, Church and Society's commitment to peace, and the UN and International Affairs ministry based in New York's CCUN, are the fruits of this earlier board's labors. Its ministries continue to promote nuclear disarmament; peace; and international, multilateral agreements across nations and societies.

The Board of Social and Economic Relations

The genesis of the Board of Social and Economic Relations in 1952 marked a difficult and tense moment in the history of the church and

6. "Commission on World Peace," *Doctrines and Discipline of The Methodist Church, The Methodist Publishing House,* ¶1291, 1940.

7. "Methodism's Board of World Peace," Guide to the Administrative records of the Division of World Peace of the General Board of Church and Society 1916-2009, General Files 1936-1960, Board of World Peace Historical – 1951-1952.

wider U.S. culture. In the U.S., the rise of McCarthyism stoked fears of communism's threat to democracy, drawing suspicion to justice seeking bodies. The Methodist Federation for Social Action (MFSA) was as an early caucus of the church that advocated for social justice and was instrumental in the creation of the Social Creed. It had been under severe scrutiny at the time both within and outside of the church. With the increasing controversies surrounding MFSA, the church created the Board of Social and Economic Relations in 1952 to address social issues while distancing itself from the caucus.

The Board of Social and Economic Relations addressed employment, trade, labor, and housing. It also staunchly supported racial integration and promoted democratic ideals. A. Dudley Ward was elected in 1952 as the board's executive secretary, at which time the board was based in Chicago in the same headquarters as the Board of World Peace.

At its very inception, the board leadership established an interagency committee on Christian social concerns made up of representatives from the Board of Temperance, Board of Social and Economic Relations, the Board of World Peace, as well as the Women's Division of Global Ministries. Sans the Women's Division, the coordination of the interagency group was a clear harbinger of the eventual merger in 1960 of the Board of Temperance, Board of Social and Economic Relations, and the Board of World Peace into the Board of Christian Social Concerns.

The United Methodist Building on Capitol Hill

One cannot speak about twentieth century Methodist social witness without reference to the UMB in Washington, D.C. While the architecture, financing, and storied efforts to preserve the building over the years are all significant, the UMB's culture of hospitality and community life is especially important for to understand the ministries of Methodism's social witness.

The corner upon which the UMB would be erected was, at the time, an open lot with billboards erected upon it. Rev. Dr. Clarence True Wilson, General Secretary of the Board of Temperance, Prohibition, and Public Morals, spotted the corner property and had a vision for a welcoming place where Methodists could influence societies and government. Dr. Wilson brought Board President Bishop William McDowell to the site, and, as Bishop McDowell recalls, Dr. Wilson pointed out how the location was close to the Capitol, Library of Congress, and Senate Office Building. The U.S. Supreme Court Building that is now situated next to the UMB had not been developed yet.

The property was acquired through the generous donations of many Methodists, particularly Methodist women. In 1923, the cornerstone was laid for the UMB and construction concluded with a dedication on January 16, 1924. In 2016, the General Conference designated the UMB a Heritage Landmark, a designation that according to the *Book of Discipline* is for "a building, location, or structure specifically related to significant events, developments, or personalities in the overall history of The United Methodist Church or its antecedents."[8]

The vision for the building that Dr. Wilson articulates centered on upholding public morality and curbing addiction. At the building's dedication service Dr. Wilson declared that the building was presented: "in order to make more effectual the efforts of the Church to create a Christian public sentiment which will relate the principles of the gospel of Christ to the economical, political, industrial and social relations of life."[9]

While encouraging public witness, the building was also designed to be a meeting place for Methodists, visitors to the Hill, Congress, the Supreme Court, and government officials. In 1936, the Woman's Christian Temperance Union (WCTU) and Methodist bishops held offices in the building.

In 1931, the adjacent 110 Maryland Ave. building broke ground and was originally designed as apartments for those in the surrounding Capitol Hill area. By 1953, the building was truly a center for community life. In a report to the Annual Meeting of the Board, J. E. Joiner reported that in addition to the Board of Temperance offices, the building held the of-

---

8. General Commission on Archives and History n.d.

9. The Dedication of The Methodist Building 1924.

fices of The Bishop of The Methodist Church, Washington Area; The District Superintendents of the Baltimore Conference; and The Methodist Commission on Chaplains. A chapel, dining room, laundry facilities, and 67 apartments were also on site. Three Methodist Bishops; twenty-one U.S. Senators; U.S. Representatives and others connected with Congress; ten Library of Congress employees; and seventeen government employees, including two from Supreme Court (one a Justice) all occupied the apartments during this time.[10]

Today, the Methodist ecumenical and interfaith commitments continue to be reflected via the New York UNIA ministries at the CCUN as well as within the UMB. At the time of this publication, the 110 side of the UMB comprises both apartments and offices. It has provided housing for interns of color during the summer, visiting speakers and consultants, and Church and Society staff. U.S. Representatives, ecumenical offices, and interfaith offices all occupy the complex. The General Commission on Religion and Race as well as the Council of Bishops and United Methodist Women held offices in the building in recent years. For faith groups and ecumenical partners who bring groups to the Hill to learn about issues and to advocate with decision makers, the building's conference rooms and chapel are made available and affordable when many other spaces in the area are cost prohibitive for non-profits.

To see the building's ecumenical and interfaith occupants today as simply a diminishment of mainline Protestantism in America is to overlook the many ways that the building's activities, programs, and partners reflects the Board and its predecessor bodies' commitment to peace and justice.

At the same time, the impetus for creating the building was in part an explicit Protestant claim to assert its role and agenda on Capitol Hill. The legacies of racism, sexism, colonialism, anti-Catholicism, and anti-Semitism cannot be ignored in the construction of the building, even as the Commission of World Peace and other sister agencies called for peace, ecumenical understanding, and the "brotherhood of man" were explicitly named by the Commission of World Peace and other sister agencies at the

---

10. Joiner 1953, 14-15.

time. The building's construction included Black laborers, presumably at very low and inequitable wages. The Methodist Building's dining room was racially segregated until the summer of 1947 when Bayard Rustin and the Fellowship of Reconciliation visited the building's dining area and met with leadership to change the policy.[11] Furthermore, Washington, D.C., sits on the ancestral lands of the Nentego (Nanticoke) along with the neighboring Indian tribes of the Piscataway, Pamunkey, Mattaponi, Chickahominy, Monacan, and Powhatan.[12] Yet, at the dedication ceremony of the Building, there was no recognition of colonialism's past and ongoing effects on Indigenous peoples in the area. Finally, one can find anti-Semitic and anti-Catholic sentiment related to the Board's early temperance agenda.

Just as we lament the offensive language used in the past by authors published by Methodist agencies, we also lament the harm inflicted by these legacies of racism, colonialism, and xenophobia. Methodists believe in a gracious and redeeming God, and we pray that the building's current and future work will continue to make amends for its sins that have caused harm and prevented the flourishing of all.

Church and Society continues to enable United Methodists and our ecumenical and interfaith partners to come and stand on Capitol Hill for justice and shalom. Public officials and decision makers pass the building every day and, through the building's events and messages, are called to a higher law of love and justice for all.

The 1972 Social Principles

By 1972, the EUB and the MEC had merged, and the Central Jurisdiction of the MEC was dissolved. Globally, at the time of the 1968 merger, the Sierra Leone missionary area of the EUB denomination merged with the UMC. The Philippines Central Conference determined it would also continue to be part of the UMC. The Methodist Church in

---

11. "Citizen Group Drafts Interracial Proposal on YMCA Coffee Shop," *Evening Star*, Washington, DC, July 25, 1947, A-7.

12. American Library Association 2019.

Cuba became autonomous along with all other Methodist churches previously under the Latin American Methodist Central Conference.

Each of the predecessor bodies had developed its own understanding of moral and social life, as had many denominations and ecumenical bodies throughout the first half of the twentieth century[13] The challenge was to take the social statements of each body and to develop a proposal that reflected the composition of The United Methodist Church.

As a temporary measure, the 1968 *Book of Discipline* simply included both the EUB and MEC's social witness documents concurrently. The two sets of social teachings would need to be merged somehow to create one document.

The Evangelical Association and United Brethren Social Teachings

In the 1968 merger, the EUB brought a strong tradition of anti-discriminatory, anti-racist positions related to church life, economic justice, the sacredness of the sabbath, and personal and familial moral life. Born from the Evangelical Association and united Brethren Church, the EUB was smaller in numbers than the MEC, was located mainly in the northern part of the United States, and its membership was largely born from German immigrant roots.

The moral and ethical orientation of the EUB traditions up to the early twentieth century emphasized the importance of family life and holy Sabbath. Divorce was permitted only on the grounds of adultery, for example. Sunday was not a day for labor, and temperance as well as abstaining from tobacco were also foundational to a life of faith for the EUB tradition.[14]

In 1909, the General Conference of the United Brethren Church approved a report of the Committee on Moral Reform and adopted a social creed inspired by the Federal Council of Churches. As historians J. Bruce Behney and Paul H. Eller write:

---

13. For more on the history and origin of the Social Creed tradition (Gorrell 1988).

14. Behney and Eller 1979.

This social creed marked a new chapter in the life of the united Brethren Church, separating the earlier day with its almost exclusive accent upon personal morality when the Christian responses to poverty and social injustices were prayers and alms. Earlier thinking added to the call to individual Christian living the presumption that society stood in need of overhauling, even Christianizing, and that Christian men and the church bore responsibilities for achieving this end. . . . God's redemption is available for individuals and social relations. The world is his by creation, and by dedicated efforts, human society may be shaped into his Kingdom, or at least into something approximating it.[15]

With clear influence from the Social Gospel movement, the United Brethren Church emphasized building the Kingdom of God on earth.

Later in 1933, the United Brethren Church revised its social creed. It dissolved its social agency, called the Commission on Social Advance, to form the new Social Service Commission. The Social Service Commission lasted until 1945 when the Commission on Christian Social Action was formed.

While not fully funded, the Evangelical Association's Board of Public Morals had been formed in 1930. While the evangelical tradition adhered to a moral life that emphasized a "personal commitment to Christ," the Evangelicals broadened their social teachings in part due to economic realities at the time: "Out of the deep anguish of the Depression years had come a more profound understanding of the worth and dignity of every human being whose right to justice was God-given."[16] By 1934, the Evangelical Association churches were advocating for economic justice including "minimum wage laws, programs of profit sharing, old age pensions, and government ownership of natural resources."[17]

In 1946, when the two denominations merged to become the EUB, they approved a new social document called "Basic Beliefs Regarding Social Issues and Moral Standards." It addressed six areas of major social concern: (1) Church and Economic Life, (2) Community Life, (3) Family

---

15. Behney and Eller 1979, 248.

16. Behney and Eller 1979, 349.

17. Ibid.

Life, (4) Moral and Social Conduct, (5) Racial and Cultural Relations, and (6) World Order. This document served as a "foundation on which the new Commission built its work."[18]

The Methodist Episcopal Social Teachings

In the 1970 interim report of the Social Principles Study Commission, they also relate the history of the Methodist Church and social concerns. The adoption of the 1908 Social Creed developed out of the work of the Methodist Federation for Social Action (MFSA). The Creed's early iteration was in part a response to the rising industrialization of the late nineteenth and early twentieth century. It called for many economic measures to address ill-treatment of workers and the plight of poverty, calling for unemployment insurance, restrictions on workdays, and the right to collective bargaining. Protections for children and the aged were also part of the Creed. Over the course of the twentieth century, the social concerns expanded to include race relations, the United Nations, alcohol and drugs, use of natural resources, and population.

At the time of the 1968 merger, the Social Creed of the ME Church reflected five main areas: (1) The Family, (2) Economic Life, (3) The Church and General Welfare, (4) Human Rights, (5) Peace and World Order. For the Commission, they saw the Social Creed tradition as prophetic and perpetually speaking to the era in which Methodists were facing: "its ideals have bequeathed an enormous responsibility to those in the Church now dealing specifically with social action. The Creed challenges the Church's leaders to be equally energetic, prophetic, and astute in their anticipation of the issues on which the church must speak and act in the remaining years of the Twentieth Century."[19] The Commission at the time emphasized the need for the proposed document brought to the 1972 General Conference would carry the legacy of prophetic and astute language forward.

---

18. Social Principles Study Commission 1970, 871.

19. Social Principles Study Commission 1970, 876.

Racial Justice and the Study Commission

Systemic racism in Methodism's polity and social actions hovered over the Study Commission's work, and its work depended on leadership that would guide the UMC through racial divisions that had been previously codified in the 1939 merger of the MEC, North, and the MEC, South. It was an uneasy compromise that involved the creation of the Central Jurisdiction, a racially segregated structure for Black churches and Black leadership.

By 1964 with the rise of the Civil Rights movements, the Methodist Church was pressed to address its racially segregated structure. As Bishop James S. Thomas recounts,

> From the beginning it became clear that the 1964 General Conference would do something significant about the Central Jurisdiction. In their Episcopal Address, the bishops spoke in unequivocal terms[:] "We are dedicated to the proposition that all men are created equal, all men are brothers, and all men are of eternal worth in the eyes of God. Prejudice against any person because of color or social status is a sin." And even more pointedly, "We believe that this General Conference should insist upon the removal from its structure any mark of racial segregation and we should do it without wasting time." This will cost some Negro Methodists some of their minority rights. It will cost some white Methodists the pain of rooting out deep-seated and long-held convictions concerning race relations. But God Almighty is moving toward a world of interracial brotherhood so speedily and so irresistibly, that to hesitate is to fight against God and be crushed.[20]

That same year, Bishop Thomas was received into the new North Central Jurisdiction and assigned as bishop of the Iowa area of the North Central Jurisdiction. It was one of two newly integrated jurisdictions in the denomination. Leading up to the 1968 General Conference, Bishop James S. Thomas was instrumental in negotiating the terms of the dissolution of the Central Jurisdiction, offering amendments to reports to chart a path forward.

---

20. Thomas 1992, 115.

Social Principles Study Commission

As part of The Plan of Union, the denomination developed a Study Commission to develop a new set of principles: "There shall be a Social Principles Study Commission, appointed with authorization to study Part III of the Plan of Union and to bring to the General Conference of 1972 a recommendation concerning The United Methodist Church's statement of social principles."[21] The Commission met together and sought to integrate the previous social statements into one document for The United Methodist Church.

Bishop James S. Thomas, given his leadership over the course of two previous quadrennia negotiating and navigating the complicated work of racial reconciliation, was elected chair of the commission. Notable civil rights activist Rev. James Lawson was part of the interim working group.

The 1968 Study Commission's overall membership reflected constituents from the former Central Jurisdiction, the EUB, and the MEC.

- The EUB was represented by the Vice-Chair, Dr. C. Willard Fetter, along with Dr. Wilmert H. Wolf, as part of the working group.

- For the MEC, Rev. A. Dudley Ward, formerly chief executive of the Methodist Board of Christian Social Concerns and now General Secretary of the newly named General Board of Church and Society, led the working group.

- Two women served on the commission, one as the secretary, Mrs. Ted F. Baun (Alice), and the other Mrs. John Gridley (Dorothy).

Certainly, the commission did not reflect the full life and lived experiences of United Methodists of the late 60's. Representation of Black women, Indigenous peoples, persons with disabilities, LGBTQ communities, Asian Americans and Hispanic Americans as well as United Methodists living outside the United States were not part of the commission.

---

21. Social Principles Study Commission 1970, 869.

Nevertheless, it was a step toward creating a more inclusive vision of the denomination's leadership and future.

The Commission's Process

As of 1970, the Commission had solicited papers and positions from a variety of perspectives. Out of the sixteen persons invited, four thought partners represented Methodism globally:

- Dr. Querubin D. Canlas, chairman of the Philippines Central Conference Board of Social Concerns

- The Rev. K. H. Voigt, minister from the Federal Republic of Germany

- Rev. Julio R. Sabanes of the Methodist Church in Argentina

- And Mrs. Sarah B. Adams, member of the Commission on Social Concerns, Monrovia, West Africa

Theologians and social ethicists from a variety of U.S. seminaries were also invited to participate:

- Dr. Philip Wogaman (Wesley Theological Seminary)

- Dean Walter G. Muelder (Boston University)

- Dr. C. Eric Lincoln (Union Theological Seminary)

- Dr. Roger L. Shinn (Union Theological Seminary)

- Dr. George Crawford (Southern Methodist University)

The Commission also undertook a series of hearings in the first half of the quadrennium in each of the five U.S. jurisdictions, and people were encouraged to submit papers in response to what was presented. The 1970 interim report found that there were "persistent issues" across all of their research, including "racism, peace, family and economic life, alcohol, or drugs." The document also needed to address "emerging new areas" such as "environmental pollution and population problems."[22]

---

22. Social Principles Study Commission 1970, 880.

In addition to the variety of input received by scholars and others, both denomination's social documents certainly informed the development of the 1972 Social Principles. Out of these hearings and position papers, the Commission curated a team of writers, and a final draft was presented to the church in 1972 General Conference for consideration.

The new 1972 Social Principles document was created with six sections: (1) The Natural World, (2) The Nurturing Community, (3) The Social Community, (4) The Economic Community, (5) the Political Community, and (6) the World Community. The first section on The Natural World reflected a heightened awareness of the need for a section dedicated to the environment.

When the Study Commission introduced its report to the 1972 General Conference, Melvin Talbert (later to be elected a bishop in 1980) presented the report alongside Bishop Thomas. He noted that a "theme" of the new document was community: "When we recognize that it is within the various communities that we find ourselves, we are challenged to work out of our existence. We may describe these as natural communities, or human communities."[23] Thus, the nurturing, social, political, and world sections all include the word *community* as part of the section, with the only exception being the first section entitled "The Natural World." Talbert suggests that the group understood each grouping to be marking a relationship where the responsible person is challenged to practice Christian action. Bishop Thomas similarly indicated that the statements in the Social Principles were intended to "give meaning to the crucial areas in which human beings struggle and sometimes die."[24] The principles are designed to aid the church and its members in these different forms of community on the crucial issues of the day.

The Commission's goal in developing the principles was to create a document that was succinct, comprehensive, and relevant to the age: "One of our major difficulties was the attempt to make this document short enough, yet comprehensive enough to be usable, and this we have sought faithfully to do. Instead of such a lengthy document, the Com-

---

23. 1972, 289.

24. 1972, 290.

mission sought to speak as clearly as we could to certain areas of life that are crucial in the 1970's." The document had to be clear, brief, and yet substantive.

The principles also needed to serve their purpose apart from more specific language used in the resolutions: "The Commission defined its task as that of setting forth principles general enough to be the basis of more specific resolutions, yet specific enough to leave no doubt as to the subject under consideration."[25] To do this, they avoided writing extensively on topics, however tempting it may be. "If the Commission had attempted all the elaborations they desired to do, on such subjects as drugs and war, it would be presenting a document that would be at least three times as long as the present document."[26] Thomas' reference to drugs and war illustrate the sign of the times. During the early 1970's the United States faced the harsh realities of the Vietnam war while promoting the federal War on Drugs campaign, the latter of which was eventually considered a deleterious program that disproportionately impacted Black and other marginalized communities. One can imagine the desire to speak more on war and addictions beyond a statement of principle in such polarizing times.

However, the era was not completely obfuscated from view in the drafting of the principles. Two areas in which the Commission shifted from its inherited documents included criminal justice reform and racial justice. In the Methodist Social Creed, the concerns for criminal justice were expanded to reflect a "broader interpretation" of the "administration of justice" to include that of the prison system and the ways that the poor are disproportionately prosecuted.[27] Thomas also gives an example related to human rights within the creed. He notes there are three paragraphs in the EUB document that address racial and cultural relations. The Study Commission recognized the importance of those words yet decided that, for the current era, the Commission needed to address the rights of women, youth, ethnic minorities, and children.

---

25. 1972, 291.

26. Ibid.

27. Ibid.

After much hard work over the four years, the document was brought to the floor of General Conference by the Legislative Committee on Christian Social Concerns and presented section by section for a vote. Amendments were proposed by delegates on many issues, including but not limited to divorce, women's equality, persons with disabilities, homosexuality, abortion, population, and military service.

In the end, the document was adopted and has been used ever since across the church to guide its work on issues of the day. Church and Society continues to understand the Social Principles as a central document in educational settings, and in advocating for peace and justice in the world.

In 2012 General Conference, Church and Society once again set about to reflect upon and reconsider the purpose and issues of the Social Principles moving into the twenty-first century. Just as the 1972 Social Principles Study Commission sought to speak prophetically to the era of the 1970's, the Revised Social Principles work of Church and Society sought once again to make sure that the Social Principles—while amended and refined over the years—reflect a global connectional church.

The Revised Social Principles process aimed to make the document more succinct, global in nature, and grounded in Scripture. Following the 2016 General Conference, the Social Principles Task Force of Church and Society, headed by Dr. Randall Miller with the staff support of Rev. Neal Christie and others, prepared to bring a revised Social Principles document to the 2020 General Conference. Six writing teams met followed by a period for public comment. Over 30 Annual Conferences held conversations, along with seminaries, theological schools, agencies, and caucuses. Central Conferences held consultations as well from European, African, and Filipino members. Following its round of consultations and feedback, an editorial team led by Rev. Dr. Mary Elizabeth Moore composed a final document that was then passed by the Board's directors and submitted as legislation under Rev. Dr. Susan Henry-Crowe's leadership to the 2020 General Conference.

The revised Social Principles sought to reduce redundancies, provides more uniformity in structure across the various sections, and explicitly connects the principles to the denomination's Wesleyan heritage. Human rights, social welfare, and care for creation with attention to marginalized people is a key aspect of this revision.

A Methodist Witness

The UMB on Capitol Hill, the social teachings of the church and the predecessor bodies' contributions on peace, economic and racial justice, and temperance reflects a church committed to social witness. In this tradition, Church and Society continues to witness, to resource, and to accompany those who stand for God's vision for God's people—where indeed justice will "roll down like waters, and righteousness like an ever-flowing stream" (Amos 5:24).

Leadership of the General Board of Church and Society and Its Predecessor Bodies

- Rev. Dr. Clarence True Wilson (1910–1936), Board of Temperance, Prohibition and Public Morals, Board of Temperance

- Rev. Charles F. Boss, Jr., (1924–1960), Commission on World Peace, Board of World Peace

- Dr. Caradine R. Hooton (1936–1963), Board of Temperance; Board of Christian Social Concerns

- Rev. A. Dudley Ward (1953–1960; 1963–1976), Board of Social and Economic Relations, Board of Christian Social Concerns

- Rev. Dr. George Outen (1976–1981), Board of Church and Society

- Dr. Haviland C. Houston (1982–1987), General Board of Church and Society

- Rev. Dr. Thom White Wolf Fassett (1988–2000), General Board of Church and Society

- Mr. Jim Winkler (2000–2014), General Board of Church and Society

- Rev. Dr. Susan T. Henry-Crowe (2014–2022), General Board of Church and Society

Chapter One:

Health and Wholeness

The ministry of Methodists including Dr. Clarence True Wilson and Dr. Caradine Hooton demonstrate early twentieth-century Methodist commitments to address not only the consumption of alcohol, gambling, and other drugs but also to address the root causes as they understood them. They were leaders in the larger prohibition movement, advocating for the Eighteenth Amendment of the U.S. Constitution that banned alcohol sales in 1917. Methodist commitment to prohibition was founded on addressing not only the personal comportment of the individual but also the social mechanisms that drove the sale and purchase. The 1929 report to the Board of Directors, found below, calls for enforcing the law with sellers of alcohol and other drugs as well as buyers. This commitment to address social concerns through legislative policy with an eye to developing healthy societies free of war and violence carries through today.

After the repeal of the Eighteenth Amendment in 1933, the church continued to address alcohol and other drugs. A yearly November campaign called "Commitment Day," for example, encouraged congregants to make a pledge abstaining from alcohol. At General Conference 1952, for example, the Bishops Address by Bishop Kern applauded the Board of Temperance for its work and cited that there were 3,000,000 names of Methodists pledging total abstinence from alcohol.[1]

---

1. The Episcopal Address of the Bishops of the Methodist Church to the General Conference 1952.

Notably, the temperance and prohibition campaigns of the Methodist church at the time committed to hiring dedicated staff for young people, Indigenous communities, and Black communities. There is lively debate in current scholarship as to the effect of Prohibition on women, indigenous peoples, and Black Americans. Scholars such as Dr. Lisa McGirr argue that the campaign and rhetoric used during Prohibition functioned as a blueprint for later twentieth-century regressive policies including the war on drugs. Others including Dr. Mark Lawrence Schrad argue that Prohibition was linked to other freedom movements including abolitionists and suffragists, wherein marginalized communities were active leaders. Freedom movements saw Prohibition as part of a larger agenda, he argues.

In 1914, Dr. John Nelson Clark Coggin was the first Secretary of Colored Work of the Board of Temperance, Prohibition and Public Morals. Dr. A. R. Howard later held the post. Both engaged in programming related to the temperance movement with Black Methodist churches in the United States. Indigenous leaders were also featured in the temperance movement. In 1951, *The Voice* featured a story about Rev. George Braswell of the Cherokee nation. It reported that Rev. Braswell was sent to pastor the Cheyenne, and while he was there, he fought against the sale of alcohol and bootlegging even as he faced violence and intimidation by others in the community.

It is important, however, to consider the ways that minority leadership was impacted by white supremacist structures. Within this volume, for example, Black leadership in higher education comment on the temperance movement in an article entitled "Negro Leaders on Prohibition," published in 1930. One might consider how the voices of Black leadership were constrained by racist realities in society and the church. On the one hand, the article allows for the voices of Black Methodist leadership to be evident in this influential paper. On the other hand, how might their comments have been different if they were spoken free of an atmosphere of racial violence, discrimination, and a Jim Crow system of law?

While the Board was concerned about the ways alcohol and other drugs impacted the family, particularly women and children, a concern for the health and flourishing of women and children continues to this present day. In the middle of the twentieth century, the Board advocated for family planning support to be part of aid to developing countries as a way of curbing over-population and strain on the earth's resources. Since then, human rights advocates have raised the right of bodily autonomy, particularly when it might restrict human freedom. However misguided such a policy might be, the desire to support women and families on the margins to be healthy and flourish has continued to be part of the church's work.

As early as 1975, the Board was raising support for federalized health care access for all. In 1977, the Board opposed the adoption of the Hyde Amendment restricting federal funding of abortions, arguing that everyone should have the same access to abortions regardless of economic status.

In the 1970's through the early 1980's United Methodists organized an infant formula task force. The task force called on Methodist boards and annual conferences to join secular partners in boycotting Nestle and its subsidiaries. This global movement was concerned about how companies were marketing infant formula to developing countries in a way that resulted in misuse and malnutrition to infants.

Attention to cigarette smoking among youth continued to be part of the concern for the health and wholeness of young people. The Board joined a boycott against Philip Morris in the late 1990's for targeting young people in their marketing to use tobacco products. Rev. Jane Jull Harvey testified before Congress in support of the cigarette tax during the 1990's.

Organ donation and developments in genetics have been important issues the Board has addressed as well.

In the early 2000's through the dedicated efforts of Rev. Cynthia Abrams, Bishop Leontine Kelly, and others, United Methodists were able to successfully support the historic passage of the Affordable Healthcare Act in 2010. It was a landmark piece of legislation that expanded access to healthcare for millions of Americans.

Into the later part of the twentieth century, the Board continued to be concerned about issues of addiction and violence. In 1992, The United

Methodist Program on Substance Abuse and Related Violence (SPSARV) was enacted to respond to the Bishop's Initiative on Drugs and Drug Violence. In the mid-1990's, SPSARV sent a delegation to Ghana to understand their program for addressing substance abuse. In 1994, a delegation from Northern Europe came to the UMB to collaborate on addressing substance abuse in their context.

With the HIV/AIDS pandemic in the mid-1980's, the realities of global pandemics became a central concern for the organization. *Christian Social Action* published a special issue dedicated to the AIDS crisis in 1986. Advocacy to support public health efforts during the Ebola outbreak in 2014 was an important intervention in public policy. In 2020, worldwide access for a vaccine to help mitigate the COVID-19 pandemic's ravaging effects was critically important.

In a world beginning to emerge out of the COVID-19 pandemic, there are rising concerns for mental health and suicide prevention in communities. Methodists are again mobilizing to respond.

Looking back on this history, one can see that Methodists have advocated for the health and wholeness of society throughout the twentieth century up to the present day, continuing to live ever more into its commitment to address the flourishing and peaceful shalom of all communities and especially those most marginalized.

"Twentieth Annual Report of Clarence True Wilson," Clarence True Wilson, *The Voice*, 1930

(From Meeting of the Board of Managers, December 4, 1929)

Our Board has a wide field of activity and does a great many things but it has never stepped out of the boundaries marked out by the three-fold landmarks of its name. It is a Board of Temperance, Prohibition and Public Morals of the Methodist Episcopal Church. In serving the three purposes, thus indicated it remembers that it is "of a Church." It is not, therefore, a political organization nor a business organization nor a social organization nor a mere agitational movement, but it is to represent the mandates of the Church in three departments of the Church's own activities.

. . .

It Is a Board of Temperance

It defines temperance to be the moderate use of all things that are useful and right and total abstinence from what is known to be hurtful and wrong. Our Board has carried on for twenty years a consistent and persistent educational campaign for total abstinence from all habit-forming, irritant, narcotic drugs, including alcohol. And we have never emphasized this more effectively than during the present year when our Secretary for Colored Work has furnished a leadership with an amazing success in advocating total abstinence pledge-signing among the young people of his race in colleges, high schools, day schools, Sunday Schools, in Sunday meetings, lodge lectures, convention addresses, and street speeches. The wording of the pledge has caught the imagination and appealed to the heart and conscience. It is a study in the art of putting things. I give it:

"Believing that the drinking of intoxicating liquor does our people great harm and no good, and that I should loyally stand by the Constitution of my country, and set a safe example before others—I pledge, God helping me, in honor of the sacred thirst of our Lord and with the help of His Holy Spirit, never to drink intoxicating liquor or to use any narcotic or opiate, and that I will through life exert my utmost endeavors to prevent their sale and use by others."

Prohibition

The time came when the Temperance Society of the Methodist Episcopal Church had to be organized into the Board of Temperance and Prohibition because the temperance work and workers came to the culmination of their work in the destruction of the saloon. The Church was just as much at home in fighting the liquor traffic as it was in rescuing the individual drunkard and saving the personal drinker. There have been various people, generally on the other side from us, who are exceedingly anxious that the Church should keep to the personal work of rescuing the drunkards and saving the sinners, but do nothing about the conditions that make these characters. . . . If I had to prove to the world that the Church of Jesus Christ is not dead or dying or recreant or indifferent to the world's needs, I could think of no more striking example that it is alive and alert, conscientious and constructive as to present day needs, than its recent historic adventure in committing itself with all its interests and influence, its popularity and its prospects to the prohibition of the liquor traffic in the United States and its announced program of extending it around the world. . . .

Public Morals

Our Board became the committee of the General Conference for the carrying out of its public morals program at the session of 1916, where large functions were delegated to it—such as the education of the young people of the Church on the amusement question, the standing for the Church's ideals in love, marriage and divorce, the defense of the Church's standards on the use of tobacco for the young and the defense of the laws that had been enacted to protect the extreme youth from the insidious poison of the cigaret [sic], the insistence on the moral standards in the movies and codes of decency in the theatre, the re-establishment by law of the prohibition of prizefighting in the several states, the revamping of moral ideals that must take the place of the looseness, lewdness and lawlessness that followed as the aftermath of the war, a teaching as to the philosophy of reverence based on the close relationship between religion and morals.

Religion and morals are one. Religion is morality toward God; and morality is religion toward men. They are not in separate compartments in our nature and they are not to be kept separate in human life. The Church can never escape its responsibility for the moral life of the community. There is no such thing as preaching religion and letting the morals of the community alone. Preaching the Gospel as Jesus did would get a greater grip on civic conditions, moral standards, personal character and political life than the way we are doing it now. The Gospel according to John the Baptist, or as Paul preached it will always smite wickedness in all places. . . .We are in the aftermath of the World War. One of the terrible things about war is its utter slump in public morals. All wars have the same effect. They break up home life, church ties, community standards, [and] take men from family restraints and put them in abnormal conditions where they are in proximity to unrestrained evil. . . . America must show the world how to get rid of its two most dreadful scourges—rum and war. Within the nations, no rum; between the nations, no war. We are working out both these problems slowly but successfully. The nations are adopting a plan for a warless world, and if we do not fail to help God answer our own prayers, the dream of Lincoln will come true:—"And when the victory shall be complete – when there shall be neither a slave nor a drunkard on the earth—how proud the title of that land which may truly claim to be the birthplace and the cradle of both those revolutions shall have ended in that victory. How nobly distinguished that people who shall have planted and nurtured to maturity both the political and moral freedom of their species."

. . . We must have no backset on prohibition at any time. It is entitled to as fair a chance and as long a time to show the world what it can do as the license system had. It has never had a fair chance until now; it never could have till we elected a President on the direct issue of a strict and impartial and uncompromising observance and enforcement of prohibition. We have a man who will not sit in the White House swivel chair and see the Constitution of our country trampled upon by a gang of aliens who affect to despise us, and a set of home-born renegades who repudiate their Puritan birthright for the mess of pottage to be gotten through the impuritans who have organized to take possession of the land.

Must Punish the Buyer as Well as the Seller

Logically those who make the distinction between the individual act of drinking and the public act of selling must see that the paying of money for bootleg liquor is as much of the part of the sale as the giving of bootleg liquor for the price. . . . We shall bring booze back when they show us

For Justice and Enduring Peace

who NEEDS it and OUGHT TO HAVE IT. Is it the automobile drivers or the aviators; the railroad engineers, all under Rule "G"; or our college boys; the women of our homes or our children? In the old days, a farmer told his Kansas legislature: "I have seven good reasons for sticking up for prohibition—four sons and three daughters."

The needs of our time are summed up in these lines:

Mental suasion for the man who thinks,
Moral suasion for the man who drinks,
Legal suasion for the drunkard maker,
Prison suasion for the statute breaker.

"Negro Leaders on Prohibition," *The Voice,* 1930

The following article is a compilation of statements from Black Methodist leadership on how Prohibition has impacted their campuses and communities.

The Department of Colored Work of the Board of Temperance, Prohibition and Public Morals, Dr. A. R. Howard, secretary, has just concluded an investigation as to the opinion of Negro leaders on prohibition. The statements of these leading Negro citizens are significant in the highest degree and particularly significant are the statements from the presidents of Negro educational institutions:

Mrs. Mary McLeod Bethune, President of Bethune Cookman College, says, "The majority of the student body are in favor of the Eighteenth Amendment; since prohibition more students are enrolled and there is decidedly less drinking and crime among Negroes."

Dr. J. B. Randolph, President of Claflin University, says: "The students are in favor of the Eighteenth Amendment. From my own observation, there is comparatively no drinking now. Drunkenness was common before prohibition. Now drinking is rarely seen. Prohibition has not increased crime among Negroes. The Negroes are a negligible quantity as violators of prohibition laws (in the nation as a whole). Prohibition has not accomplished all that we desired, but there is no doubt that conditions

28

are marvelously improved since prohibition went into effect. Not only is there more sobriety, but more decent living, more self-respecting men and women, better homes, higher standards of living, more thrift and saving, more domestic happiness, more peace and public safety, in these prohibition days."

Dr. M. W. Dogan, President of Wiley College, Marshall, Texas, says: "The student body believe in and support the Eighteenth Amendment. The attendance has increased since prohibition, there is no drinking that I know of among students and bills are paid more promptly. Crime has not increased among Negroes since prohibition. There are better homes and the people are more reliable as a result of prohibition."

Dean Kelly Miller, of Howard University, says: "I do not think prohibition has increased drinking. Prohibition has had great effect on the home life of the Negro. Economy is shown in money saved from cost of drink."

Dr. Judson S. Hill, President of Morristown Normal and Industrial Institute, says: "The students are favorable toward the Eighteenth Amendment. There is absolutely no drinking that I know of among students. There is increased attendance and the bills are more promptly paid. There is decidedly less drinking, thus decreasing crime among Negroes. They are happier, have better homes and more money is saved."

Dean W. T. B. Williams of Tuskegee Institute, Alabama, says; "Drinking among students is negligible. Prohibition has not increased crime among Negroes. It has made possible greatly increased funds for use in the home and so has increased home comforts. It has also greatly improved deportment among Negroes."

Dr. W. A. Fountain, President of Morris Brown University, says: "Prohibition has decreased crime by 70 per cent, it has decreased poverty and suffering, it has made more Negroes thrifty and developed a better home life; it has developed the moral and ethical code."

Bishop W. A. Fountain, of the A. M. E. Church, says, "Prohibition has been of incalculable benefit to our group. The industrial and social atmosphere of the community life is purer and more children are having an opportunity to attend school."

"Dr. C. R. Hooton Supports the Johnson-Case Bill, at the Hearings," *The Voice*, 1952

Editor's Note: The following is testimony that the General Secretary Hooton made at a Congressional hearing opposing liquor advertising

I appear before you as President of The Council of Secretaries of The Methodist Church. The Boards and Agencies which I represent are composed of well-equipped administrative leaders who are entrusted with the moral and spiritual development of many millions of members and constituents.

In the discharge of this sacred commission we conceive it to be our privilege to help people to achieve better standards of good citizenship. For the realization of more wholesome living, we devise techniques which prepare persons for intelligent participation in orderly social progress.

For the mental and physical growth of its young, America today supports the costly operation of 193,878 schools. Two hundred fifty-three thousand, two hundred seventy-six churches maintain intensive programs for the moral development of creative personalities. People of this nation sacrifice large sections of their income to make possible for children and youth the advantages of scientific and spiritual cultures.

And yet we license some 483, 633 outlets for narcotic drugs, and spend more than twice as much for ethyl alcohol as for ethical advancement. We expend huge sums for cultural education and double this financial strain to tear down, all too soon, what schools and churches have labored unselfishly to build up for human welfare. Does it make sense to invest one dollar in activating the brain, only to spend two dollars to put it to sleep again?

The most powerful educational agencies today are those which present their appeals through colorful pictures and dramas.

Brewers and distillers have capitalized upon this. Parents can teach some selectivity in regard to glamorous magazine and billboard enticements, but when they invade the sacred confines of the innocent home by way of the radio and television, the power of pictorial suggestion is altogether too great. New customers for alcoholic beverages are being rapidly made, even among the children, to whom, incidentally, it is still illegal to sell alcoholic beverages of any kind. Have you gentlemen weighed the frightful consequences upon youthful character of such an unexplained inconsistency? We can legally create appetites which we make it illegal to satisfy! But childish familiarity with brands and favor of products is being so rapidly established by the Beverage Alcohol Traffic, that already in Chicago surveys show that more than fifty percent of the city's teenagers are users of alcoholic intoxicants.

This unethical appeal is reaching little children as well. One of my little four-year-old friends recently pranced across the room with her glass of orange juice, just as a well-known TV program flashed a view of people drinking beer. Although she had never tasted the beverage, she smacked her lips, sang the beer song, and holding up her glass, said, "Good, just like Blank beer."

To evaluate the effect of advertising upon men's appetites, the Coca Cola Company discontinued all advertising for one month. Their sales fell off 60%. Through the elimination of liquor advertising, homes can once more become the centers of training for Christian citizenship and tomorrow's leaders can face life with clear heads.

"Population Growth and Human Well-Being," *Concern*, 1964

Editor's Note: Part of a movement that saw global population growth as a threat to peace and stability and encouraged family planning as a response to economic development.

From the article: A Paper Prepared by a Policy Committee of the General Board of Christian Social Concerns of The Methodist Church, recommended for study.

Introduction

Think of over ten billion people per square foot of land on earth! That would be the population pressure on the resources of the world today if the present growth rate of two per cent per year had been occurring since the time of Christ!

The total world population of more than three billion people is now growing at a rate that will more than double our world neighbors before the end of this century. Our children born today must prepare to live with ten to twelve billion neighbors. The problem of an exploding global population is new in human history. Never before has mankind faced the terrible prospect of famine, unrest, and war on such a massive world wide scale.

What is the responsibility of society in permitting this cycle to continue? What is the role of the Church? What can be done to prevent suffering and to meet the basic needs of the world's people?

When a sower goes forth to sow he does not crowd as many plants together as would be physically possible. Instead, he considers the spacing necessary if more adequate plants are to grow—whether in the field, forest, or family garden. God's action in nature has helped man to learn the wisdom of stewardship and planning in natural resources. So has God's action in human living helped men and women to learn the wisdom of stewardship and planning in the improvement of human life, in the home, the community, the nation, and the world. There are many aspects of this stewardship, but perhaps none is more crucial than the concern about population growth and its threat to human welfare. Throughout most of the history of mankind the population has grown at rates far below 2 per cent each year. The unprecedented rise to a global annual average of 2 per cent and even 3 to 4 per cent in some countries has been the result of modern health services, social organization, and education.

Man now rejoices in the prevention of death and the prolongation of life achieved by science. Further achievements will continue the dramatic drop in death rates. Every family and government on earth seems driven to find new ways to prevent death and suffering. Christian institutions have led in extending the values of health and long life throughout the world, as an outreach of Christian mission and an expression of Christian love for all mankind.

While we welcome the saving of life, we must now face changes in the balance of nature that will demand unprecedented adjustments in our customs and patterns of living. The physical space and resources of this world will not permit all of us to live in abundance if the present rate of population growth continues indefinitely.

The question is: Will man decide voluntarily to promote stewardship in "birth-making" to compensate for the advantages sought through life saving? Or will men unknowingly promote "death-making" through starvation, epidemics, or war?

More than half the babies born this year will not have enough to eat. Many of these babies were not wanted by their parents. It can now be considered a mark of irresponsibility on the part of society or lack of parental love to let children come into the world when there is no chance of providing for their needs. The great masses of impoverished mankind have high birth rates simply because they have neither the information nor the means to control their fertility. Many mothers want relief from constant child-bearing. Many fathers are distressed because they cannot provide adequately for the children they have.

Many people of the world are deprived by law and religious restrictions of knowledge and equipment that could help them plan for the number of children they want in their families.

The problem is not just population growth but also concern for the cooperative relationships between human need. Human goals do not center on how many lives can be produced, but rather on the quality of living, both spirit and material, for all mankind. It is technically possible to feed more people. But man lives by more than bread alone.

It is our Christian responsibility to focus attention on the need for making better use of resources that are potentially available to meet human need, even if this requires revising former customs, traditional beliefs, and forms of social organization.

Gap Between Nations

If the earth's resources were distributed evenly throughout the world, if people were free to move from crowded areas to less crowded areas, and if all people had equal opportunities to get an education and find remunerative work, the problem would still be difficult. But with earth's resources so widely varied, with historical national boundaries being used to avoid sharing opportunities and resources with others, and with the existing barriers to equality and opportunity for the people of the world, the population pressure is critical.

The gap between the rich nations and the poor nations of the world is increasing. At the same time, poor nations have the world's highest rates of population growth. We have shared our health revolution with the poor nations. We are only beginning to share the technology of our production revolution. We forget that the rich nations of the world started the capital accumulation for their industrial revolution while their population was growing at less than 1 per cent per year. Poor nations with a growth rate of 2 to 4 per cent per year find it difficult to acquire enough savings to build their homes, schools, hospitals, and public service facilities.

Where will they find the investment needed for improved agriculture and other forms of productive development? People in the more privileged and wealthy nations aspire to continue higher levels of living, drawing upon the talents and resources of underdeveloped and impoverished areas of the world like a magnet. Meanwhile, the poor areas of the world are unable to acquire the capital and resources they need as fast as their population is growing. Poverty and despair must follow.

If people in the wealthy nations remain blind to this global imbalance, the poor nations will have recourse to desperate measures of social revolution and totalitarian controls in attempting to meet their needs.

The Threat of War

With the technologies now available, a small number of people could bring death and destruction to a developed area of the world without evidence from whom or where it came. Materials for chemical and biological warfare are available at small cost. All the military might and power in the United States could not defend us against a determined series of acts of non-conventional violence. The only hope of preventing it rests in an all-out effort to be sure that no group of people in any part of the world will have sufficient deprivation or grievance as to resort to this kind of desperate violence.

There is no chance to make an all-out effort against poverty and in-equality of opportunity for the future well-being of mankind and for pre-vention of the anonymous war, without achieving a break-through in the population-economic development race.

Meanwhile the population explosion confronts the entire world like a tidal wave. But man could control the population explosion if collective knowledge in fertility control, demography, and social organization now available were applied in every area.

Uncontrolled world population pressure in the near future will call for a lowering of immigration restrictions as well as a systematic organization of public revenues to provide minimum food, education, health services, and other public needs for people throughout the whole world.

Voluntary measures to deal with the individual family problem as well as the global problem will help to assure that we will not be confronted with totalitarian reorganization of world population and distribution.

Goals for Development

The Universal Declaration of Human Rights, adopted by the United Nations, includes the following among its thirty articles:

"Article 1: All human beings are born free and equal in dignity and rights. They are endowed with reason and conscience and should act to-wards one another in a spirit of brotherhood.

"Article 25: (1) Everyone has the right to a standard of living adequate for the health and well-being of himself and his family, including food, clothing, housing and medical care and necessary social services, and the right to security in the event of unemployment, sickness, disability, wid-owhood, old age, or lack of livelihood in circumstances beyond his con-trol."

These are general goals and represent values which are familiar to Christians who have taken their biblical heritage seriously.

These goals impose special economic burdens, social and political obligation on new nations which did not confront the older nations during the period of development.

United States and Population Policy

It is well known that the United State has been reluctant to become involved in any public-supporting policy related to birth-control programs. Although it has supported demographic studies and research in certain types of fertility and birth related problems, it has carefully avoided dissemination of drugs or material devices for human contraception.

But there are indications that the United States believes the time has come to develop a blueprint for international cooperation to deal with the world population problem.

Deputy Assistant Secretary of State for International Organization Affairs, Richard N. Gardner, issued a statement of US Policy in December, 1962. The statement called for expanded research on population trends and alternative methods of family planning. It encouraged the United Nations to (1) assist member governments to obtain factual information on the demographic aspects of their economic and social development, (2) training of nationals for demographic work, and (3) the promotion of discussion of population problems. In a succeeding statement in May 1963, Mr. Gardner said: "Countries seeking help—should have access to the wide variety of sources of assistance available throughout the world. While the US will not advocate any specific family planning policy to any other country, we can help other countries, upon request, to find potential sources of information and assistance on ways and means of dealing with population problems, the provision of materials for this purpose can best be done by those government whose citizens are not divided on this question, by private foundations, and by business firms." (Dept. of State, *Foreign Policy Briefs*, 5/27/63).

This reference to "government whose citizens are not divided on this question," reflects the religious differences that keep the United States from supporting national or international projects for the promotion of birth control.

While nations that are confronted with the needs of large scale technical assistance and materials for promotion of family planning are asking for help from the US and the UN, the resistance and lack of understanding among religious people in the United States is the main reason for the delay in meeting those needs.

A New Mission

The Christian churches have led in extending education and health services to the people of the world. This challenge has been taken up by the governments and foundations to provide for continued improvement of health condition and services for mankind.

The churches are now confronted with another need, which in a sense has grown out of the previous success of the health mission. This is the need for helping people understand how they can help plan for the children they want, and how their stewardship of God's resources is affected by population growth, as well as by production, distribution, and conservation of goods and services. Let the Christian churches lead in this new mission, and welcome the cooperation of all people who are concerned for the abolishment of poverty and starvation throughout the world. Let this be a practical fulfillment of the biblical calling for feeding those who are hungry, healing those who are sick, meeting the needs of even the least, and loving our neighbor.

To perpetuate beliefs that bring unwanted children in a world unable to care for them is wrong against both the child who suffers, and the community that must bear the burden of diluting its meager resources.

The time has come for thoughtful religious leaders to recognize that the existence of certain religious beliefs is a major barrier to voluntary family planning and social population policies that assure the meeting of basic human need throughout the world.

Most of the world's religions are not opposed to birth control. The Moslems, Hindus, Buddhists, and Confucianists have not doctrinal reactions on control of conception. The Roman Catholic position presents the only major theological obstacle to population control. Political leaders have been understandably fearful of pressures from the Roman Catholic community.

Now encouraging signs appear which point to a softening of Roman Catholic intransigence in the near future. Catholic voices have been raised favoring fertility research and calling for the removal of restrictions on birth-control advices in medical programs. Roman Catholic theologians are reminding their people that responsible parenthood requires parents to weigh medical, economic, and social factors and to limit their families accordingly.

Protestants should welcome every opportunity to develop interfaith consensus. Public exchange of views on platforms, in publics, on radio, and in television debates will bring clarification of issues and an awakening of public conscientiousness to the need for cooperative action on this critical problem.

As Reverend John A. O'Brien, research professor of theology at the University of Notre Dame, explained in articles published simultaneously in the Catholic weekly Ave Maria and Protestant weekly *Christian Century* (10/28/63 and 11/6/63): "The revolution in the ethical thinking of Protestants has occurred with such speed that many Catholic seem unaware that contraception is no longer seen in Protestant eyes as an evil thing, but may be a good, virtuous and even holy action, demanded by the changed conditions of modern life and commended by the vast majority of physicians."

"It is time," Father O'Brien declared, "For Catholics and non-Catholics to meet together to discuss the population problems, analyze their points of agreement and difference, and solve the problem in a way that will respect the conscience of all."

Action by the Church

The people in the Churches could take the following steps in relation to the world population problems:

1. Urge full United States participation in the programs of the United Nations by various agencies, which assist the member nations in dealing with population growth.

2. Urge the federal government together with public and private agencies, to mount a vastly expanded program of research on fertility control, as well as problems of community organization and communications related to lowering the birth rates.

3. Urge the federal government to implement fully its avowed policy extending technical assistance in support of fertility control programs to those countries requesting it. The church should support use of foreign aid funds for this purpose, while opposing restrictions which would force countries to organize population control programs as a prior request to receive foreign aid.

4. Encourage church groups and private organization to study the facts about population growth and the steps needed to relieve widespread problems of poverty and deprivation.

5. Urge all church-related hospitals to provide family planning services to patients who desire assistance.

6. Train all missionaries with the skills and equipment needed to offer family planning services when requested.

"National Health Insurance," Grover C. Bagby, e/sa, 1975

Editor's Note: This editorial discusses proposed legislation—the Health Security Act—that would provide comprehensive health insurance for all.

Economic hard times bring critical looks at all aspects of a society. The current recession has a multiplier effect on whatever inequities there are—inequities that we tolerate more easily, however unwisely, in better times. One current illustration concerns health insurance.

The bulk of the population under sixty-five in the United States is covered by job-related health insurance (although not all businesses offer such coverage), so when the job is lost, the health insurance is also lost, usually after a period of thirty days.

The thirty-day extension period theoretically provides an opportunity for the newly unemployed person to shift to individual policy coverage. The theory is faulty on two counts. First, because individual policies are significantly more expensive than group policies, and pay benefits on an average of only 50 to 55 per cent of premium income. A great bulk of American working families, however, will not find themselves able to pay for health insurance even at a reasonable cost, during a time of unemployment.

For over a decade there has been a slowly growing recognition in this country that all is not well with the methods by which we finance and deliver health care. The newly uninsured, unemployed have added new point to this growing recognition.

. . . It is time for the Congress and the country as a whole to enter seriously into the discussion over the question of a rational and equitable health insurance plan for the nation, and a rational system for establishing cost and quality controls in connection with the delivery of services.

So far in this Congress two of the major national health insurance proposals of the last Congress have been reintroduced. The Health Security Act has been reintroduced with some improvements, in the Senate by Senator Kennedy (S. 3), and in the House by Congressman James C. Corman (D., California) (H.R. 21). . . .

The AMA is expected to throw its weight behind the Administrative Bill that President Ford says he will introduce in January 1976. The president indicated that he would veto any new big spending programs this year. It is expected that the Health Insurance Industry Bill will also be introduced later in this year. . . .

In any case, the Kennedy-Corman Bill, (the Health Security Act) is judged by the Board of Church and Society of the United Methodist

Church, and by a number of other denominational agencies and boards, to come closest to fulfilling church-espoused principles for health care reform. These principles are set forth for United Methodism in the 1972 General Conference Statement entitled "Health Care." . . .

The question is, why go through all this if the President would veto the bill anyway? The answer is: because the country needs such a program; because a presidential veto might be headed off, if popular support develops and an aroused public opinion expresses itself at the White House; and because even if a veto is issued and sustained in Congress, the public and the Congress will have studied and debated the issue in depth.

This is not to say that H.R. 21 or any other bill can be a panacea. When old problems are solved in any dynamic area of social existence and human well-being, other problems arise. But some problems can be alleviated or bettered, if not solved, and that's why this Congress needs to try to do in the health care field the best it can. The question is, will the Congress put band-aids on the infections, or will they trot out a relevant and effective therapy?

"There Is Another World 'Out There'" Allan R. Brockway, *e/sa*, 1977

Editor's Note: This article presents a call for United Methodists to write decision makers about the Hyde Amendment and its implications for health-care of low-income women. Dear Representative _____: I understand that Congress will soon be considering the 1978 Labor-HEW Appropriations bill with the Hyde Amendment that bans the use of federal funds to pay for abortions. Please vote against this blatantly discriminatory legislation that denies poor women legal health care services that are readily available to others. It is unjust and unfair that poor women choosing to terminate an unwanted pregnancy are denied access to legal health care. Please vote against the Hyde Amendment.

The sample letter, included in an anti-Hyde Amendment action sheet mailed out in the June "Word from Washington" packet from the Board of Church and Society, summarizes the dismay of many persons over recent congressional action on the controversial issue. Unfortunately, citizens urging "please vote against the Hyde Amendment" did not have the impact (or make the noise) on vote-conscious representatives that the militant (and loud) anti-abortionists were able to generate. When the House finally acted on the Hyde Amendment, 201 representatives voted for it, 155 against.

Last year Congress got into the same hassle over abortion when the Labor-HEW Appropriations bill came up and finally adopted a compromised Hyde Amendment that prohibited use of federal funds to pay for abortion *except when the life of the mother was endangered*. However, in October, a federal district court issued a preliminary injunction against carrying out the Hyde Amendment on the grounds that it was unconstitutional, discriminatory, and violated equal protection of the law. Appealed, the case had been pending before the Supreme Court, but on June 29 the Court ruled against the injunction, in effect opening the way for enforcement of the 1977 Hyde Amendment.

Further congressional action on the question of using federal funds to pay for abortions also occurred June 29 when the Senate voted to forbid such use except where pregnancy would endanger the mother, abortion was determined to be "medically necessary" by the woman's doctor, or was caused by rape or incest.

Since that language differs from the House-passed ban on all abortions, a House-Senate Conference Committee will work out compromised language. But it appears certain that the final bill for fiscal 1978 will have an anti-abortion provision, probably as potentially restrictive as the present one, now seemingly free of injunction.

. . .

As the pages of this and other United Methodist publications have indicated in the past, our denomination holds no consensus about abortion. Some of us advocate the woman's unlimited right to decide. Others of us walk with the right-to-life advocates, denouncing abortion as life-destroying. Many others of us are wrestling to discover our opinion on complicated questions revolving around abortion.

We United Methodists, however, are not without foundation stones on which to base our stance. Our Social Principles states: "We call all Christians to a searching and prayerful inquiry into the sorts of condition that may warrant abortion. We support the legal option of abortion under medical procedures." More directly, a "Resolution on Responsible Parenthood," adopted by the 1976 General Conference encourages "our churches and common society . . . to safeguard the legal option of abortion under standards of sound medical practice, and make abortion available to women without regard to economic status."

Without regard to economic status. We can only achieve that principle without restrictive measures such as the Hyde Amendment as well as others that the determined anti-abortion campaigners will attempt to foist on our society.

We are not at all convinced that the frightening clamor set off by anti-abortionists represents majority opinion. We believe, instead, it's a raucous minority. They remember too well how Joshua noisily fought the battle of Jericho. So it comes down again, as all the critical controversial issues do, to the raw, tedious act of political organizing for efforts to achieve through our legislatures the goals we think will best serve that "world out there." In other words, we need to strengthen the efforts "to safeguard the legal option of abortion," and particularly to make abortions available to women "without regard to economic status."

"A Review of the Continuing Effort to Resolve the Infant Formula Issue," Anita Anand, *e/sa*, 1982

Editor's Note: The article reflects the work of Methodism in response to the global crisis of infant formula misuse.

From the publication: Anand was the program coordinator in the Department of Peace and World Order, United Methodist General Board of Church and Society, and also a member of the United Methodist Infant Formula Task Force.

May 21, 1981, in Geneva, Switzerland, the World Health Assembly (WHA) took a ground-breaking vote. The member nations of the WHA, by a vote of 118-1 (with three abstentions), adopted a far-reaching Code of Conduct that sought to encourage breastfeeding and restrict the promotion of commercial infant formula products and other breast-milk substitutes.

Adoption of the Code came after a two-and-a-half-year process, initiated by the World Health Organization (WHO) and UNICEF, that involved health experts, consumer groups, the formula industry, and government representatives. The US government stood alone in casting the single negative vote against the Code. Argentina, Japan, and South Korea abstained.

Defending the US position in a column published in *The Washington Post*, Assistant Secretary of State for International Organizations said: "The US government reached the decision to vote 'no' after two years of unsuccessful efforts to make this Code less rigid and after days of hearings. . . . Because of its provisions, the United States could not . . . and would not . . . wish to enforce the Code, here at home, so we have reached the conclusion that we cannot in good conscience vote in favor of it."

On June 16, 1981, the US House of Representatives passed House Joint Resolution 287 expressing dismay at the US negative vote on the Code of Conduct. The vote was 301-100 (with two of the members voting "present" and twenty-eight members not voting). Two days later the Senate passed an amendment to the State Department authorization bill, expressing "concern" at the US vote on the Code. The amendment won unanimous support except for Senators John East (R-NC) and Steven Symms (R-ID); nine senators were absent.

Misuse of Infant Formula

What was it about this issue that compelled Congress to oppose the Administration in this manner? At the heart of the Code lies the infant formula controversy. Brought to the attention of many church groups around 1974, the controversy focuses on the acute malnutrition suffered by babies in the Third World. This malnutrition occurred because of misuse of infant formula aggressively marketed and promoted by infant formula manufacturers.

With data from several parts of the world where socio-economic conditions did not permit the safe use of infant formula (heating/refrigeration facilities, running water), two organizations, Interfaith Center for Corporate Responsibility (ICCR) and Infant Formula Action Coalition (INFACT), charged that industry was "killing babies." Bottle contamination and formula dilution (resulting from inadequate basic facilities and misuse of formula) led to diarrhea, malnutrition, and ultimately death.

Industry, when challenged with these facts, responded in various ways. Some companies changed their practices, some said they had changed their practices, and others denied the charges. In 1977, INFACT organized a boycott against all Nestle products and its subsidiaries. The boycott was called partly because the US company is a subsidiary of the Swiss-based company and is not accessible to the same shareholder action that US-based companies are. ICCR began to file shareholder resolutions at the meetings of three American companies: Abbott Ross, American Home Products, and Bristol Myers.

For years ICCR and INFACT, along with the International Nestle Boycott Committee (INBC), made up of representatives of various institutions endorsing the Nestle Boycott, have tried to negotiate with industry. The efforts have achieved varying degrees of success.

With Nestle, there have been a series of acts in good (and bad) faith, leading to little agreement on the issues of the boycott. Marginal progress including some changes in marketing practices has been made with the American companies.

Drafting the Code

In 1979 the WHO and UNICEF began to put together a Code of Conduct on the marketing of breastmilk substitutes. For the first time in the history of international negotiating, WHO/UNICEF brought together as equals health professionals, industry and government representatives, and consumer groups to draft the code. Companies like Nestle felt that this would be a good forum to work out, at an international level, any differences related to the boycott.

As time went on, however, industry began to withdraw from the process. As the Code reached its final stage in late 1980, industry was prepared to withdraw completely.

When the Code was passed in May 1981, Nestle stated that it intended to support the aim of the Code, but could not adhere to all parts since it conflicted with marketing practices in some countries. Nestle did agree to work with each government to ensure that proper policies were set up and followed. In the past when Nestle has been challenged with reports of violations documented by the critics, the company spokespersons have responded by saying that the data is unscientific and cannot be verified. They also explained that certain practices terminated by Vevey (Nestle headquarters) were continued by their subsidiaries over whom they have no control. While this is a reality, it also represents an "easy way out."

The three US companies campaigned against the WHO Code, lobbying Congress and the Administration through the Grocery Manufacturers of America (GMA). Former North Carolina senator and GMA lobbyist Sam J. Ervin wrote in a *Washington Star* article (May 13, 1981): "The draft Code regulates with complete, drastic and totalitarian precision every aspect of the marketing, distribution and using of infant formula products in foreign nations subject to it and defines with equal precision every permissible activity of every person involved in any way in such transactions."

Recommendation to Nations

Ervin's interpretation deliberately distorts the aim of the Code, a *recommendation* (not regulation or law) to the member nations of the WHO to use the Code as a *minimum* to design legislation as a protection against commerciogenic malnutrition caused or exacerbated by commercial activities. Framers of the Code are sensitive to the fact that member nations have different political, social and economic systems; they encourage adoption of the Code as it suits each country.

The companies argue that the Code does not apply to the United States since conditions contributing to formula misuse do not exist; that

Code activities will violate the anti-trust provisions of US business regulations; and that in good faith the United States could not vote for something it believed it would not and did not need to follow. These assumptions of the companies could be challenged. Breastfeeding among women in the lower socio-economic strata in the United States is declining, especially among poor, white, Hispanic, Black and Native American women.

In communities all over the United States, women of child-bearing age are working full-time outside of the home. These women, should they choose the breastfeeding *option*, face a lack of facilities. Workplaces should have child care centers where lactating mothers can keep their children and breastfeed them at least for the first year.

Local churches can play an important role in this effort. If women are expected to provide the best nutrition (breast milk) for the newborns, then it is society's responsibility to provide an environment that makes breastfeeding an optimum choice. Cultural mores often discourage women from public breastfeeding.

For many women, work has become necessary to support themselves and their dependents. Single family homes are increasing. Women could be forced to opt for infant formula due to work/economic pressures. Care must be taken not to make these women feel guilty over the decision not to breastfeed.

UM Infant Formula Task Force

The 1980 General Conference of the United Methodist Church mandated the denomination's General Council on Ministries (GCOM) to appoint a task force to study the infant formula issue and report no later than July 1982 to GCOM. The nine-person task force has been working since October 1980—studying, discussing, and meeting with individuals and organizations involved in the controversy. A preliminary report was made to the GCOM meeting in October 1981. The General Board of Global Ministries (Women's and National Divisions) and the General Board of Church and Society have endorsed the Nestle boycott. When the Board of Church and Society endorsed the boycott in 1979, its resolutions urged all church members to study and act upon all aspects of the controversy, as

47

individuals and as a community. Thirty annual conferences have endorsed the boycott as well. What does this mean for our work on the issue, and more importantly, what does this mean for our lives and work in general? The infant formula issue highlights many valuable lessons:

- Decisions regarding people's lives cannot be made in the boardrooms of corporations in Mexico, Paris, New York, Geneva, or London. People supposed to benefit from the products that corporations produce and market should have an input into the process.

- Community resources go into the planning, marketing and consumption of all goods and services. Since these resources (money, raw materials, time and energy) are not unlimited, wise and discriminatory decisions regarding their use must be made.

- In the case of infant formula it is not just the ethics of marketing of formula that is in question. The questions to be asked are: Is the formula needed? By whom? How will it be used? How much will it cost (individually and societally)? Under what conditions should it be produced? Who should produce it?

These questions cannot be left simply to the corporations to answer. They require a forum where all affected (women, men, health professionals, community workers, researchers, government officials and corporate leaders) will be represented. The WHO/UNICEF process came closest to providing such a forum. This could be duplicated at a local state and national level.

The churches have been put in a highly polarized situation. Whose side should they take? Is endorsement of the Nestle boycott endorsing the notion that all corporations are bad? Does refusing to endorse the boycott mean that corporations are all right and/or that critics' demands are not legitimate?

It would be good to move away from an either/or position to gain some perspective on the issue. What exactly does endorsement of the boycott mean? It means lending solidarity to the groups calling for the boycott as a means of pressuring the industry to behave responsibly. It recognizes the fact that a corporation is a powerful entity that should be responsive to consumer needs and challenges—responsive, that is, for reasons other than mere face-saving.

In the case of the infant formula issue the extremely powerful corporations have been pitted against the powerless, the poor, their uneducated mothers and their babies. The role of Christians and the church in such a controversy is to understand first the complex aspects of the issue through study, discussion, anzd debate. In moving to action, and relating it to our daily lives, it means exercising our powers as individuals in a community to attempt to make the necessary changes.

"Alcohol Use and Abuse: A Family Affair," Bishop Felton May, *Christian Social Action*, 1994

Editor's Note: Bishop Felton May worked actively on issues of health throughout his episcopal tenure. This article highlights his work relating to drug and alcohol use.

From the article: This article is excerpted from testimony presented by Bishop Felton E. May of Harrisburg, Pennsylvania, on March 31, 1993, before the twenty-four-member President's Commission on Model State Drug Laws charged with developing recommended legislation dealing with use and abuse of drugs.

Our young people . . . consume alcohol because they see their parents drinking. If mom and dad do it, then it must be all right, despite mom and dad's warnings to the contrary. Alcohol use and abuse is a family affair.
. . .
In community after community, neighborhood after neighborhood, across the United States, drug addiction very clearly claims more than addicts as its victims. When one or both parents are addicted, their children and other family members become victimized by this insidious disease.

Grandmothers Become Mothers

What happens to these children? In thousands of families, grandmothers become mothers again as they assume the primary responsibility for their grandchildren whose parents are addicted or have been killed through some violent act. Without the loving care of these dedicated—but overworked—women, we would be facing even more tragedies of abuse, neglect and even the deaths of these young children.

The toll on these women is enormous. According to the US Census Bureau, 3.2 million children in the United States live with their grandparents—an increase of almost 40 percent in the past decade. Systemic issues related to AIDS, legal problems, lost values, miseducation, poverty and substance abuse have caused millions of the elderly to assume important child-rearing responsibilities.

Drug addiction doesn't care if you're African-American, European American, Native American, Asian American, or Hispanic American. Addiction doesn't care if you're poor, middle class or rich. Despite this knowledge, drug use is most commonly portrayed as an African-American issue, an inner-city phenomenon involving illegal drugs bought and sold by persons with little money.

Parents Influence Children

Let me give you an example of how this stereotype is just plain wrong. Alcohol is the drug of choice for the vast majority of Americans. In many families, the mothers and fathers don't know what influence their before-dinner martinis are having on their children.

I was in Edmonds, Oklahoma, participating in *Born Free/Stay Free*, an excellent drug education/ prevention program. . . . During our session with parents from this upper middle class suburb of Oklahoma City, a woman asked how she could get her daughter to obey her orders to not use drugs. She said, "I keep telling her not to drink or use drugs, but she turns to me and says back, 'But you use them everyday.' The mother's response was: "I'm the parent. You are the child. I give the orders. What I say is what counts. What I do isn't your business."

This mother was perplexed and in pain. She could not understand how her daughter would react in such a way.

"I'm the parent. She's the child. It's none of her business what I do." She asked me for my reaction. I could give her none then, for her addiction had taken over. She couldn't see that her disease was setting up her daughter to become an addict herself. The question was asked, "Will you as this child's mother give up drinking and drug use so that your child will have a healthy role model?" The mother dropped her head and she did not answer. Only tears came forth.

For this family there was hope, because the mother and daughter would at least begin to communicate through their involvement in *Born Free/Stay Free*. Most parents and children in addicted and co-dependent situations have not had access to that type of assistance.

The Community as Family

. . . We need to talk about the community as family. We need to talk about the need for each of us to be responsible for our neighbors' well-being, and the consequences if we don't take that responsibility. We must become our neighbor's neighbor.

In Shade Gap, Pennsylvania, a tiny community located about 90 miles west of Harrisburg, members of the community began to overcome their silence, their co-dependence. Their motivation was simple: too many young people were dying because of drug-related causes, and it was clear that drugs were as easy to buy in Shade Gap as in any city.

Meeting in the town's fire hall at the behest of a United Methodist layman, Bill Bair, the community, acting as a family caring for all its members, formed the Shade Gap Drug Task Force. One of the first things the task force did was to develop a "Statement of Support for a Drug-Free Community" and seek commitment from the 147 families in Shade Gap. In that statement, families agreed not to use illegal drugs, to safeguard the use of prescription drugs, and to consider alcohol as a drug. A hotline was created for reporting illegal drug activity and a community education program was developed, with free counseling available.

Of the 147 families in that community, 142 signed the statement. More importantly, to show their commitment publicly, each family placed a sign in their front yard. It's been nearly three years since that first meeting, and the community remains active in this effort. Why? Because persons overcame the co-dependency to begin to understand the disease and face it head on. It was a family taking care of its brothers and sisters.

Practicing "Misericordia"—"Misery of the Heart": The HIV/AIDS Ministry of the "Juan Wesley" Methodist Church, Rev. Dr. Juan G. Feliciano-Valera, *Christian Social Action,* 1999

Editor's Note: Toward the end of the 1990s, the HIV/AIDS epidemic had become better understood, but it remained a stigmatized disease due to the prevalence of the disease in the LGBTQ community. This article highlights how Church and Soicety's board of directors were part of the ministries reaching out to create spaces of hope for those impacted by the disease.

From the article: Rev. Dr. Juan G. Feliciano-Valero, pastor of "Juan Wesley" United Methodist Church, Puerto Rico, was executive director of the HIV/AIDS Support Committee for three years and a member of the General Board of Church and Society.

The north health region of Puerto Rico (Arecibo), to the northwest of San Juan, is comprised of 14 towns and cities. It has a large number of persons infected and affected with HIV/AIDS (or PLWA, People Living with AIDS). Puerto Rico, as a whole has had over 18,000 cases of HIV/AIDS reported and, if considered among states in the US would be the third largest in HIV/AIDS cases. Ten percent of those cases are in Arecibo.

Although the number of deaths has decreased significantly (as a result of expensive medications), a large number of new cases are reported and treated in Puerto Rico each year. Arecibo is one of the regions with a large number of new cases. A lack of effective education for prevention, treatment, compliance, compassion, and outreach programs contribute to the increase of HIV cases.

. . .

Compassion and Justice Ministries

Pastoral care for PLWA and their families have included compassionate companionship, crisis intervention with families, special worship services at the church (most broadcast over a regional AM radio station, WMIA), participation in special events for advocacy, radio and TV appearances, funerals, and memorial services.

The need for spiritual support cannot be overestimated.

The Living God, Creator, Redeemer, and Sustainer has always been with those oppressed, marginalized, rejected, the poor, the sick, the discriminated against, the needy. In Latin and Spanish, the concept of "mercy," or "kindness," (found often in the Bible) is *misericordia*. This is a concept composed of two words: *Miseri* (meaning misery, suffering, oppression, tribulation, etc.), and *cordia* (related to the heart; "cardiology," "myocardial," etc.). In Jewish and Christian Scriptures, this concept represents the empathy, the identification, the invention, the preference of God for those in pain or misery, the hopeless, abandoned, discriminated against, rejected by society, etc.

These people, created in God's image, "by the same hands that created you and me" (Mother Teresa) are the "modern" lepers. Among them, PLWA are eminent. The Greek concept for *misericordia* includes the notion of the womb, a shelter, and a refuge; God, Father and Mother, with loving care, sheltering God's children. I count myself as one of the "grateful ones." My ministry is driven by my gratitude to a God who is willing to descend and liberate the oppressed (Exodus 3). My model is Jesus, the Christ, who suffered all sickness upon himself and raised victorious with Hope, Grace, and Peace with Justice for all God's children.

"Better Health Care, A Special Christmas Gift to Americans," Rev. Cynthia Abrams, *Faith in Action*, 2009

Editor's Note: Rev. Cynthia Abrams was the Director of Health and Wholeness who worked on advocating for healthcare for all. The advocacy efforts of Church and Society contributed to the passage of the Patient Protection and Affordable Care Act (ACA) in 2010.

Several months ago, I received an email from a United Methodist whose husband had learned he was losing his job and employer-based health care in the economic downturn and she pleaded with me to let Congress know that they didn't know how they were going to be able to receive the health care that was necessary.

A few months ago, my nephew (and godson) was in a major traffic accident when the car he was in was rear-ended by a drunk driver. He spent three days in a trauma hospital. 5 months before the accident he was dropped from his parent's health insurance after turning 25 years of age and was ineligible for Medicaid because he also held down a job which did not provide health care while attending college to assist in his college expenses. During the 3-day hospital stay he accumulated a $97,000 bill and is in the midst of a long physical rehabilitation including major dental reconstructive surgery. His mother managed to convince her employer to add COBRA benefits for this young man at an added cost of over $1,000 per month in addition to what they were already paying for the rest of the family. My sister and her family face serious financial straits because of this accident.

A United Methodist who is an attorney and family were covered by health insurance through her law firm. She developed cancer, received needed treatment and fortunately, went into remission. A few years later, the cancer came back and the family was slated to be dropped from their health insurance. The woman faced a decision no one should have to face—to divorce her husband so that he and their children could receive health insurance.

In United Methodist Annual Conferences, the burden of rising health care costs for clergy and other church employees places an enormous strain on the financial resources of local church budgets causing churches to cut program budgets in order to provide the necessary health care for employees.

I'm proud to be a clergy member of a denomination that declares "Health Care a human right" and a "responsibility of government to provide its citizens with health care." (Social Principle 162V). I have to be candid; some United Methodists have contacted me who cannot understand why our denomination has such a position. Many think everyone ought to take care of their own health care or they cannot believe there are over 47 million uninsured. Some even want to re-adjust this count by saying some human beings in our country don't deserve health care. Frankly, I believe Jesus set the bar pretty high in reaching out to the disenfranchised among us. I disagree that some in our country ought to be able to have better health care than others.

The prophet Ezekiel denounced the leaders of ancient Israel whose failure of responsible government included failure to provide health care: "you have not strengthened the weak, you have not healed the sick, you have not bound up the injured, you have not brought back the strayed, you have not sought the lost, but with force and harshness you have ruled them" (Ezekiel 34:4). Our situation today is not unlike those faced by the prophet Ezekiel.

Our country is at a critical point in ensuring that no American will go without health care. The Senate is very close to passage of *The Patient Protection and Affordable Care Act* (H.R. 3590) The United Methodist position on health care passed by the General Conference demonstrates that the House and Senate bills are not perfect. Yet, the bill is significant because it contains far more protections for people with health care and covers far more people who do not currently have health care. The key components of the health care reform legislation are consistent with the path outlined in United Methodist Resolution 3201 which calls for support of legislation that gains greater access to health care. Furthermore, if we let this opportunity slip by, comprehensive health care reform may not be possible in the forseeable future and that would be utterly regrettable.

As a United Methodist, your Senator needs to hear from you. Many of you have answered our alerts and taken action all year long. We thank you for your commitment to health care. But it's "crunch time" and now is the time for you to call, fax or email your Senator again. Every Senator has their passions, but it is important that Senator's opposing health care reform set aside their personal agendas and think about the common good for all Americans; especially those most marginalized in our society. If your Senator already supports the bill, offer a thanks and let them know you are a United Methodist committed supporter of health care reform.

. . . Though the Senate is still negotiating key points, here are some key protections currently in the bill:

- No denial of coverage for pre-existing conditions.

- Helps people, especially those with life-threatening illnesses that require expensive long-term treatment by prohibiting lifetime or unreasonable limits/caps on coverage.

- Gives a leg up to families who face huge deductibles in their insurance plan by prohibiting exorbitant deductibles.

- If you work but your living expenses prevent you from finding affordable health care the bill creates premium assistance for people with incomes up to 400% of poverty.

- If you lose your job there is temporary health care coverage to cover you while you look for another job.

- For young people who are in college or in jobs without health care the bill allows young adults to remain on their parents' health insurance until age 26.

- For children, individuals and families who are indigent or struggle to make ends meet and qualify for Medicaid or the Children's Health Insurance Program (CHIP) the enrollment process has been streamlined.

- For families who have a father, mother, or child struggling with mental illness or addiction, the legislation mandates coverage for mental health and substance abuse recovery and rehabilitation.

- For seniors, it closes the "doughnut hole" in Medicare pre-scription drug coverage (Medicare Part D) by providing afford-able drugs at a reduced rate.

- And there are many other positive provisions in the legislation that are worthy of our support.

As Christians, Christ calls us to a higher purpose, likewise, as citizens of the United States; the preamble to the U.S. Constitution inspires us to achieve the greater good for all. It says, "We the people, *in order to form a more perfect union*, establish justice, domestic tranquility, and *promote the general welfare.*" As a government, we should and can be inspired to create "a more perfect union" and "promote the general welfare by ensuring that no person in our great country goes without health care.

"Social-justice agency calls for eradicating circumstances that lead to crises such as Ebola," *Faith in Action*, 2014

Editor's Note: The following statement was issued by Church and Society in response to the global ebola crisis, pointing to the need to address the justice issues related to addressing the epidemic.

A Call to United Methodists to Take Action: The Ebola Crisis

The magnitude of the Ebola crisis has disturbed people worldwide. United Methodists in our global connection have grieved and prayed for the nearly 14,000 people who have contracted the Ebola virus in eight countries. Almost 5,000 people have died. An estimated 5 million children are currently affected by the epidemic that has orphaned 4,000 of them.

We remain concerned that the virus continues to infect people, especially in West Africa. It has a disproportionate impact on women, both as sufferers and caregivers. The lack of accurate information and education coupled with the severity of the disease stigmatizes and increases the difficulty of response.

As we respond to this epidemic, we must consider the underlying causes that have enabled Ebola to move from a regional to a worldwide crisis. Much of the current crisis could have been prevented if medical personnel, resources and clinics had been in place to respond quickly to the first signs of an outbreak. The unjust sharing of resources has led to wanton impoverization.

Ample resources are not available to support these recovery efforts. Many Sub-Saharan African nations are under obligation to global financial institutions to allocate large portions of their national incomes to servicing their national debts. This obligation is to the detriment of meeting the basic needs of their own citizens.

In the midst of our despair, God comforts us and calls us to become involved in the solutions to the immediate crisis, and to use all available wisdom, personal commitment and political will to address the longstanding root causes that allow infectious diseases to strike, spread quickly and threaten already fragile infrastructures (Ezekiel 34).

Our Biblical and Theological Summons

Jesus Christ healed the sick (Mark 1:34), fed the hungry (Matthew 14:13), and challenged his disciples to do likewise (Matthew 10:8). Jesus rejected the belief that illness or disability was a punishment for sin, stating instead that it was an opportunity for the works of God to be made tangible (John 9:2).

Jesus healed the sick both to demonstrate his power and because the multitudes had illnesses. All illness is a claim on those who have the power to heal. Jesus fed the hungry. Hunger and poverty demand a response by those with power.

Jesus commanded his disciples to cure the sick, raise the dead, cleanse the lepers and cast out demons, not only to show that the Kingdom of God is here, but to show that the human need of God's children is a claim on God's kingdom.

What United Methodists Can Do

Commit to Pray. We encourage the United Methodist global connection to lift up prayers seeking God's grace for all those affected by the Ebola crisis. Pray for those suffering, their caregivers and loved ones. Pray for the health-care persons serving on the frontlines of the fight against Ebola. Pray for the work of humanitarian, development and health-related organizations, including the United Methodist Committee on Relief (UMCOR) and those serving in United Methodist–related hospitals and clinics. Pray for the World Health Organization, the Centers for Disease Control & Prevention and others working to develop effective treatments and determine best practices. Pray for the leaders of Liberia, Guinea and Sierra Leone, the nations most affected by the crisis, and for their immediate neighbors.

Pray that Christ the who calmed the storm (Matthew 8:23-27) may fill all impacted by Ebola with courage. Pray fervently and effectually that our prayers may avail much (James 5:16).

Care for the Most Affected. United Methodist churches worldwide are called to care for the ill, the dying and those who grieve. We encourage congregations in affected areas to support health-care workers and promote science-based education about the facts of Ebola and how to prevent its spread.

We further support training health-care personnel regarding local customs and cultural sensitivity to foster understanding, trust and solidarity. We must recognize that the crisis has disrupted entire societies. In many areas normal commerce has not been possible, daily life has been turned upside down, and the capacity of nations to meet their citizens' needs has been severely challenged. Crucial daily needs—needs that United Methodists uphold as constitutive of human dignity and rights of all people—

have been severely constrained. These include food and nutrition, water and sanitation, education and employment.

Abundant grace and sufficient resources are both necessary for the mobilization of political will and the resolve to address crises such as Ebola. (Learn more about the UMCOR Ebola response and how to help at Ebola Response.)

Mobilize for Advocacy. Ebola is a global crisis that knows no boundaries, and neither should our response be constrained by borders. Sub-Saharan Africa beckons with enormous need. United Methodists applaud worldwide efforts to mobilize resources, supplies and personnel. We celebrate those who have stepped forward, often risking their own safety, to serve on the frontlines in medical and humanitarian roles.

More must be done, though. The world's nations must practice life-saving generosity. Every resource to care for the ill and prevent the virus' spread must be made available.

We encourage United Methodists to advocate in their national and regional governing bodies for significant funding for the fight against Ebola. Such advocacy must also ensure that funding remains robust for other ongoing global health and development efforts. This crisis dramatically underscores the need for debt relief for the world's most impoverished nations.

We need to mobilize support for sustainable development and infrastructure that meets the needs of peoples in West Africa and beyond. These are steps toward a more just, equitable world.

The United Methodist Church must continue to join with other people of goodwill and faith to provide resources to address critical health and development challenges and be a voice of solidarity and accompaniment. We are uniquely situated to assist in these efforts because of our global connection and worldwide presence. Our prophetic call is to ensure that our eyes are looking beyond the present to achieve a better future.

Christ reminds us that we are accountable: "Even as ye have done it to the least of these who are members of my family, you have done it to me" (Matthew 25:40).

"The Need for Worldwide Vaccine Access," Linda Bloom, *Faith in Action*, 2021

Editor's Note: With the onset of COVID-19 in March 2020, Church and Society's staff urged the global community and U.S. government to support vaccine equity around the world.

United Methodist and other faith leaders view access to the COVID-19 vaccine as a human right, along with other basic health care needs.

But citizens in many countries remain unprotected from the coronavirus as multinational efforts to increase vaccine availability have fallen short. The total number of known coronavirus cases worldwide has now surpassed 200 million.

The Rev. Susan Henry-Crowe, general secretary of the General Board of Church and Society, was among the religious leaders who met virtually August 4 with U.S. Trade Representative Katherine Tai to express support for waiving vaccine patents to increase COVID vaccine access for developing countries.

"A commitment to promoting vaccine access all around the world grows out of the moral and ethical imperatives of our faith and religious traditions," Henry-Crowe said.

The United Methodist Social Principles calls health care a basic human right and a governmental responsibility. "Creating the personal, environmental, and social conditions in which health can thrive is a joint responsibility—public and private. . . . Countries facing a public health crisis . . . must have access to generic and patented medicines" (Paragraph 162 V).

The meeting with Tai was organized by Jubilee USA and Eric LeCompte, its executive director, said Tai understood the urgency of the situation. "Waiving vaccine COVID patents will help produce more vaccines and save lives in the developing world," he said.

Mark Harrison, director of the Peace with Justice Program for Church and Society, also pointed out that the COVID-19 pandemic cannot be resolved only within individual countries precisely because of its global impact.

Harrison was among the participants in a U.S. Prayer Vigil for Global Vaccine Access on July 20 at the Capitol Hill Reflecting Pool in Washington. The vigil, which also took place online, sounded an alarm over the increasing moral crisis and the setback of 30 years of development gains because of the pandemic.

In a statement read by Harrison, the Rev. Ivan Abrahams, top executive of the World Methodist Council, noted that while COVID-19 has "exposed the fault lines of global inequality," the pandemic also offers an opportunity to stand together, press reset and "work for a transformed world in which we commit to sharing resources, walking softly on the earth, and affirming dignity of all humanity."

Those attending the prayer vigil also called on the World Trade Organization to waive intellectual property rights for vaccine manufacturing in order to enable more countries to produce COVID-19 vaccines domestically, the World Council of Churches reported.

Ellen Johnson Sirleaf—the former President of Liberia and a United Methodist—raised the issue during a July 28 briefing for member states at the United Nations General Assembly, according to a World Health Organization news release. Sirleaf and Helen Clark, former Prime Minister of New Zealand, were co-chairs of the Independent Panel for Pandemic Preparedness and Response, which reported to the World Health Assembly in May.

"While in some places, vaccines are blunting the worst of COVID-19's impact, for too many countries, supplies are so limited, and prospects for access pushed so far into the future, that hope is turning to despair," Sirleaf said during the briefing.

The World Health Organization, which has called for a vaccine booster moratorium until more are vaccinated worldwide, announced August 5 that Africa reached a record peak for coronavirus-related deaths—more than 64,000—in the week ending August 1.

During the same time period, continent-wide infections rose by 19 percent, with 278,000 new cases recorded. Less than two percent of Africa's population is vaccinated.

Increased access to vaccines is crucial for countries in Africa and elsewhere, Harrison said.

"We've been thankful that President Biden has agreed to temporarily lift the patents to produce the vaccines in appropriate places in the world so people have access," he added.

That strategy, Harrison noted, was used successfully to produce HIV/AIDS medications at a lower cost, making the medications more widely available. "That's what we're trying to get done as relates to COVID."

In the U.S., Harrison said, local United Methodist congregations and individual members can take action by praying, having a better understanding of the global aspect of the COVID-19 pandemic and advocating for vaccine access.

Other countries do not have the type of rescue plan implemented in the U.S., he pointed out, and poor countries need international support through the World Bank and International Monetary Fund to recover from the pandemic and improve their economies.

"We want the president (Biden) to come up with a plan to work with the world to end the pandemic," he said.

Chapter Two:
Civil and Human Rights

The Methodist social teachings have long held a commitment to the inherent dignity of all persons made in the image of God. Out of this theological grounding, Methodists have advocated for civil and human rights. In the U.S., the history of racism has resulted in egregious violations of these rights, and the church has continued to speak out against their violation. Below can be found a statement from the Board of Directors in the 1920's stating their outrage at lynching. Methodists have also consistently marched for civil rights, not only in the famous 1963 March on Washington but also in many consequent marches—including the 1968–69 Poor People's Campaign, the 1982 call for making Martin Luther King's birthday a federal a holiday, the 1983 March for Jobs, Peace and Freedom, the 1995 Million Man March, and Black Lives Matter movement. The 1968 and 1969 Poor People's Campaign organizing team held space in the UMB to plan the massive event and call for just policies.

Racial discrimination in the criminal justice system including sentencing, capital punishment, and the police has also been of concern. Supporting local communities to address root causes of violence in their communities, police-community relations, and reforming drug sentencing have all been critical areas of work.

Native Indigenous community rights have been an important ministry for Church and Society and its predecessor bodies. In 1973, leaders of the American Indian Movement (AIM) laid siege to Wounded Knee on the Pine Ridge Reservation to demand that the U.S. government ensure fair and equal treatment of Indigenous peoples. Board staffer Rev. John P. Adams led a National Council of Churches effort to negotiate between the U.S. federal government and Indigenous leaders. The siege lasted 71 days before both sides agreed to disarm. In 1978, Methodists are reported to have supported indigenous peoples who marched across the country to the U.S. Capitol in a campaign called The Longest Walk, raising awareness and advocating for the rights of indigenous peoples in the face of deeply discriminatory federal laws.

During the 1960's, Church and Society strongly advocated for a more equitable immigration policy and continued to build partnerships and advocate for the rights of the migrant and the sojourner. Staff testified before Congress on the importance of expanding the number of refugees and immigrants allowed from non-European countries. In 1986, Church and Society highlighted the importance of addressing racial injustice for Japanese Americans. Two United Methodists, Aiko Herzig-Yoshinaga and Jack Herzig, called the U.S. government to account for its human rights violations in detaining Japanese-Americans during World War II. (Excerpts of their interview are highlighted below.)

The rights of persons with disabilities have also been a focus. In 1990, Church and Society worked in coalition to mobilize support for the passage of the Americans with Disabilities Act. Activists rallied outside the UMB for the passage of the ADA. In the 1970's, the issue of sexuality including divorce, remarriage, homosexuality, and family planning all became topics of social concern for the church. While an ongoing source of conflict, members of the denomination offered pastoral frameworks for inclusion of those who had previously been marginalized or stigmatized for their relationship to marriage and family. Women's rights were also raised from a variety of standpoints, including the intersectionality of race and gender.

One cannot underestimate, however, the ongoing level of systemic racism and colonialism that continues to play a significant role today. While the church has consistently supported the civil rights of all people, the racial disparities for health outcomes, economic life, and protection under the law continue to cause harm and prove deadly for Black and marginalized communities. The final piece in this section issued by the general secretaries of the agencies reflects a deep lament and call for dismantling the ongoing systems of racism as a central focus for the church.

"Lynching is Murder," Board of Directors, Board of Temperance, Prohibition, and Public Morals, *The Voice*, 1924

Editor's Note: This is a resolution that opposed lynching passed by the Board of Temperance, Prohibition, and Public Morals.

Whereas, Lynching is murder, an offense against God, an outrage against the right of every individual to court trial and a crime against the honor of many states and the United States, and,

Whereas, The efforts of Christian people of both negro and the white races, acting through inter-racial commissions, have materially decreased this evil,

Therefore, be it resolved, That we congratulate Christian people throughout the country on the awakening conscience of the country in regard to this sin; that we urge the extension of the principle of inter-racial co-operation and that we pledge our effort in every way and at all times to the early, entire abolition of this monstrous evil.

"A Statement on Public School Integration and Law Observance," The Board of Social and Economic Relations, 1957

Editor's Note: The following statement was adopted unanimously on September 26, 1957, by The Board of Social and Economic Relations of The Methodist Church.

The manifestations of racial hostility and lawlessness of recent days are matters of grave concern to citizens of all faiths who cherish the democratic ideals of justice, equality, and ordered freedom. We, The Board of Social and Economic Relations of the Methodist Church, consisting of laymen and ministers residing in all areas of the country, feel it to be our Christian duty and civic responsibility to speak out unequivocally during this time of moral crisis.

Defiance of law strikes at the very mainspring of democracy, and racial hatred runs counter to the fundamental Christian belief that all men are brothers, one to another. In this time of great gravity in the world situation, it is doubtful that democracy would survive the undermining and destructive effects which are the inevitable end products of intolerance and disregard for law.

We deplore the hatred, violence, and lawlessness which have been practiced by a small minority of citizens to prevent the orderly integration of public schools and the enforcement of the order of the Federal Court relating thereto. We view with equal sadness the incidents of lawlessness and racial strife which have occurred in recent months.

We uphold the hands of those leaders of government, regardless of party affiliation, and citizens who sense the terrible urgency of the issue and who are resolutely determined that the laws of our land shall be obeyed.

We recognize the complexity of integration and other racial problems and that their solution must be sought in a spirit of sympathetic understanding and with dedication to the ideals of Christianity and democracy. In that spirit we urge all members of the Methodist Church to strive unceasingly to find the solutions, mindful of our common belief in the fatherhood of God and the brotherhood of man. To do less would be unworthy of those who profess to be followers of Christ.

"They Came, They Marched, They Departed: An Interpretative Report on the March on Washington for Jobs and Freedom," Donald Kuhn, *Concern*, 1963

Editor's Note: The author offers a first-hand account of attending the March on Washington in 1963, noting Methodist participation.

On Tuesday, August 27, the day before the March on Washington, expectancy filled the air. Not since the tension-filled days of the Cuban crisis last October had Washington dwellers been so completely dominated by outside forces.

Before the March most of Washington's population did not seem to look with favor on the whole affair. Many dreaded the thought of the violence which has often erupted in hot summer months. For months columnists had predicted a climax to race struggles during the summer and usually mentioned the possibility of violence.

Not everyone feared violence. Many familiar with Congressional procedures considered the event unnecessary. They believed that such pressures on responsible legislators could actually thwart the marchers' objectives. Others did not approve of the March's objectives. Some merchants feared a drop-off in business. And some people openly expressed contempt for Negroes.

All that was the day before the March.

Then the appointed day arrived. Natives who ventured downtown at the go-to-work hour said it looked like 7:00 a.m. on New Year's Day. No parking was allowed anywhere. And the total population seemed to be composed of policemen.

By mid-morning the sidewalks bulged. As the pedestrians moved along the roped-off Constitution Avenue, toward the Washington Monument, time after time they would see a motorcycle policeman appear, followed by a convoy of ten or more buses. A quick look inside revealed happy faces. Pedestrians waved to the riders and they waved back. It was as if they were all going to a homecoming football game and knew the score before the game began. Their side was going to win.

Even before they gathered at the foot of the Washington Monument all that was going to happen that day became clear. It was etched in the evenly paced steps, the triumphant faces, the calculated dress, and the lilt of the ever-singing voices. These persons were in Washington to claim their birthrights and those of millions of other Americans who watched them. They came to petition for "jobs and freedom." Each of the marchers, by then numbering over 90,000, carried his responsibility proudly—

along with his lunch, raincoat, and his sign. They came wanting freedom. But their actions already revealed that their aim was accomplished. They were free. Their freedom did not depend on acts of Congress or the ill-defined someday of their theme son [*sic*], "We Shall Overcome."

Little by little the lawn of the foot of the Washington Monument was covered by groups assembled around signs bearing their names. Loud-speakers carried what appeared to be a random arrangement of entertainment and announcements. Folksingers Odetta and Peter, Paul and Mary performed. A few Hollywood stars were introduced. A voice announced the death of the founder of the N.A.A.C.P. and introduced Mrs. Rosa Parks, the woman who started the modern protest movement by taking an empty bus seat in Montgomery.

In this atmosphere, reminiscent of an old-fashioned Fourth of July picnic, some sat quietly on the grass while others moved around visiting with friends.

When called to prayer, the crowd numbering over 100,000 became silent—controlled, orderly, and reverent.

At about 11:00 a.m. eager marchers broke ahead of their established leaders, beginning the March half an hour early. During the next three hours the enormous crowd moved peacefully to the Lincoln Memorial.

Three types of groups filled Independence and Constitution Avenuecivil rights organizations, religious groups, and labor unions. No one segment seemed to dominate.

Many members were members of The Methodist Church. Perhaps best known participants walked behind the National Council of Churches banner. Bishop John Wesley Lord, Methodist resident bishop and vice-president of the National Council, with leaders of other denominations, led the delegation.

Behind a banner reading, "The National Conference on Religion and Race," Miss Theressa Hoover of the Women's Division staff marched.

A Methodist from New Mexico passed wearing a "United Church of Christ" ribbon. Another from Minnesota walked under a sign bearing the name of his state. Another walked with the Detroit Council of Churches representatives.

One man carried a placard reading, "W.S.C.S., Shaftsbury, Vermont." Behind him followed a woman from the same town carrying "Commission on Christian Social Concerns, The Methodist Church." She reported her District Superintendent was in the crowd some place.

Two delegations represented regional Methodist student groups. The National Conference of Methodist Youth also sent two delegations—one from the Human Relations conference in Chicago and another from the United Christian Youth Movement meeting in Ohio. Thirty students and professors came from the Methodist Theological School in Ohio. Space prohibits additional listings but Methodists participants numbered in the thousands.

Some accounts reported the March as if it were Negro motivated, Negro controlled, and completely peopled by Negroes. Yet seasoned observers estimated that about 40 per cent were not Negroes.

Most of the people came from the North and Midwest. Few, proportionately, came from the South. But there were people from Miami and Memphis. Signs read, "Tulsa, Oklahoma" and "Catholic Interracial Council of Little Rock." And often voices signing "We Shall Overcome" announced a southern group before its banner came into view. These sturdy voices tested against the roar of mobs came from Danville, VA., Cambridge, MD., and Clarksdale, Miss.

Late marchers were unable to see speakers at the Lincoln Memorial and settled down under the trees. Some, tired from long trips, fell asleep. But almost everyone listened attentively to the speakers.

All in all nothing was said which could not have been anticipated. Only twice did the formal proceedings reach a point of maximum audience response. These came after Mahalia Jackson's singing and Dr. Martin Luther King's dream. News media sought constantly to find something newsworthy. Apart from the large number of people present and their placid militancy, there was no news.

Very late, after the formal program had begun, buses full of marchers were still arriving. Finally, as they began to thin, one onlooker from Washington looked at the man standing next to him and asked, "Will this do any good?"

His companion, who had earlier reported losing a job as a waiter because he was "too dark," responded, "It has to. It has to."

Would the March have any effect on seasoned decision-makers in Congress—its primary target? If they could have watched, hour after hour, looked into each face, they would have been deeply moved. But no Congressman or Senator was seen in the March—or watching the marchers; although many found their way to the reserved seats near the speaker's stand.

Finally, the program ended. And almost as if touched by a magician's wand, everyone was gone. By the following morning there was little evidence that anything unusual had happened. From sunrise until sunset 210,000 people had entered the city, shaken the nation, and departed. Not one marcher was arrested for even a minor offense. The nation was amazed at the wonder of it all.

The March fitted into the scheme of things as a "redress of grievances"—provided by law. The least that can be said in evaluating it is that the marchers obeyed the law and they did no harm to any man.

Any further evaluation must of necessity center on the aims of the March and the method itself.

The aims (or demands) numbered ten and are as follows:

"Comprehensive and effective civil rights legislation from the present Congress—without compromise or filibuster—to guarantee all Americans access to all public accommodations; decent housing; adequate and integrated education and the right to vote."

"Withholding of Federal funds from all programs in which discrimination exists.

"Desegregation of all school districts in 1963.

"Enforcement of the Fourteenth Amendment, reducing Congressional representation of states where citizens are disenfranchised.

"A new Executive Order banning discrimination in all housing supported by Federal Funds.

"Authority for the Attorney General to institute injunctive suits when any constitutional right is violated.

"A massive Federal program to train and place all unemployed workers—Negro and white—on meaningful and dignified jobs at decent wages.

"A national minimum wage act that will give all Americans a decent standard of living. (Government surveys show that anything less than $2.00 an hour fails to do this.)

"A broadened Fair Labor Standards Act to include all areas of employment which are presently excluded.

"A federal Fair Employment Practices Act barring discrimination by federal, state, and by employers, contractors, employment agencies, and trade unions.

Realists considered these aims with understandable skepticism. Two paradoxical characteristics pervade the list—"nowness" and the improbability of their complete attainment. Both are illustrated in the demand for "desegregation of all school districts in 1963." Any person familiar with the current situation in the South would probably label the demand impossible. Yet they demanded it—and nine other changes.

Since the civil rights leaders and most members of Congress are realists, the demands listed must be considered "tactical." Some have said the intention was to cause Congress to act quickly on administration proposals—and maybe even beef them up a little.

When churchmen decided to support the March they registered the intensity of their convictions by demanding ten specific legislative or administrative changes which involve technical, legal, and economic data. They further accentuated their beliefs by making demands some of which they knew were beyond possible fulfillment now.

It is the function of the Church (1) to proclaim absolutes of being and doing and (2) to put her life on the line in support of her proclamation. In the March, the church proclaimed the right of every man to work and to be treated equally under law. She also laid her life on the line—in a mild but impressive manner.

As a method, the March was legal and advocated legal means of obtaining the goals it named. Was it successful? Only later, and then with difficulty, will the answer be completed.

Before the March, Walter Lippman predicted the passage of a civil rights bill this year—or next at the latest. So few of the results of the March will be seen in national legislation in 1963. The March may speed passage of a bill and it may change a few votes.

What the March accomplished was much more important than immediate legislation. It told the nation, indeed the world, that citizens of the United States are committed to expanding the legal provisions for freedom. They are committed to this goal with the totality of their lives— a commitment which is basically religious. They pursue their goal in a calm, orderly, democratic fashion. This message has explosive possibilities for the restricted peoples of the world and the security-fixated citizens of the United States.

The March brought together fighters from the front lines as well as some less seasoned supporters. At home they suffered from battle fatigue—or lethargy. But when gathered together in Washington with others who knew how they felt and what they wanted, a new spirit entered each person. This indwelling spirit would not be removed. The experience was more than the releasing of deeply imbedded feelings. It was the drinking in of new strength and purpose.

On August 28, 1963, a new age was born, but it was not for all men. It was for those who came, marched, and departed and those who were moved by the marchers. The New Age for all men is yet to come.

Some questions remain to be answered.

Are marches on Washington new gimmicks for exerting pressure on legislators and securing time in mass media? What will be the next big march? When will it occur?

Is this march ushering in a period comparable to Prohibition in which a vocal minority which knows how to do it brings changes in law which the total population will not support?

Does church participation in this march mark a new coalition of pressure groups which will continue to seek aggressively the passage of other social legislation?

Does endorsement of the March's aims by church leaders without passing through the "denominational consensus" stage point to new ways of marshalling the churches' social power? Does the March hold the seeds for the emergence of new schisms within the church?

"A New American Immigration Policy," J. Elliott Corbett, *Concern*, 1965

Editor's Note: The article is an in-depth analysis of proposed immigration reform and includes testimony made before Congress by Peace and World Order staff in support of the legislation.

Immigration reform, long left lapping at the poetry-enfolded feet of a certain lady in the New York City harbor, may finally be washed safely ashore by the 89th Congress.

United States immigration laws presently in force could well be the most out-dated, patched up, unbalanced, and inappropriate statutes ever to offend the sensibilities of rational men. They are out of date because they are based essentially on the national origins system established in 1924, a system that uses the 1920 census as its frame of reference.

The laws are patched-up, for, while they were revised in 1952 with some commendable changes being made, the resulting McCarran-Walter Act did not change the basic structure of the law built on the national origins system. Present policies are unbalanced because, while up to 65,000 quota immigrants are allowed into the US annually from Britain, most of the nations in Asia and Africa are limited to one hundred per year. Further, our system is inappropriate because it does not adequately reflect aboard the same concern Americans have felt and embodied in law with respect to domestic racial equality.

The need for revision of our immigration policies is evident. About half the bills introduced into Congress each year are, surprisingly enough, private immigration bills. The necessity for these attests to the fact that present legislation is not sufficiently comprehensive to provide for a multitude of pressing needs.

For example, over 3500 such bills were handled by the 87th Congress. For the most part these consist of personal hardship cases not covered by the law.

Another limitation of the present law is found in the neglect of any provision for refugees. In 1957, for instance, special legislation had to be enacted for the large number of Hungarian refugees. Following the 1958 earthquakes in the Azores, many Portuguese were left homeless. Only action by Congress, namely the Pastore-Kennedy-Walter Bill, made it possible to admit some of these destitute people to the United States. Also, when many Cubans wanted to emigrate after the revolution in that Caribbean island, special legislation was required to provide for their reception. Likewise, in 1962 a separate measure had to be enacted to allow entrance of several thousand Chinese refugees who had fled from Communist China to Hong Kong. In each of these cases, had our operating immigration laws been able to take into account such emergencies, much needless suffering and uncertainty could have been avoided.

Another most unfortunate aspect of our immigration system is that provision of the McCarran-Walter Act referred to as the Asia-Pacific Triangle. In 1952, when an attempt was made to codify all of our national laws on immigration, the complete bar against the naturalization of Japanese, Koreans, and other East Asians was removed. But at that time a system was established stipulating that all countries lying within a certain triangular land mass of Asia running from Pakistan on the west to Japan on the east, should be limited for the most part to one hundred immigrants per year. The total allowed from these countries, including most of the nations of Asia, was not to exceed 2100.

A further severe restriction provides that if as much as one-half of an immigrant's ancestors came from countries within the Asia-Pacific Triangle, he must depend, not upon the quote assigned to the land of his birth or citizenship, but to that very small quote allocated to the nation of his ancestry.

Needless to say, this extra barb of legalized discrimination had served as a continuing irritant to many Asian nations whose goodwill we have otherwise courted. In practice, other provision has meant that a prospective immigrant born in England, whose father was British and whose mother was an Asiatic Indian, had to apply for admission to the United States, not under the unfilled quota of Great Britain (65,361 per year), but under the oversubscribed quota of India (one hundred per year). The net result was that such a person under the present system, never gets into this country.

Perhaps the most objectionable feature of the currently operating immigration law is the central criteria used for admission—the national origins quota system. Through this arrangement 98 per cent of the quota immigrants must come from Europe, 82 per cent of the total being allocated to Northwestern Europe and 16 per cent to Southeastern Europe.

Since 98 per cent of the immigration quotas are reserved for Europeans, this only leaves 2 per cent for the west of the Eastern Hemisphere, mostly Asia and Africa (Persons from independent nations of the Western Hemisphere may freely migrate to the United States since they enjoy a non quota status.) Almost all of the countries of Africa are permitted an annual quote of only one hundred. This is also true for most of the countries of Asia. Friendly nations such as South Korea and the Philippines are restricted to a quota of one hundred; Japan is allowed 185.

The Philippine quota is back-logged for the next ninety years. Thus a national from these islands would have to be told by our consular representative "You may fill out this application, but I hasten to say that, under present regulations, you must wait until the year 2055." Such a policy, of course, does great harm to our international relations.

Historically, the Christian church in its world-wide operations has been a prime mover in caring for refugees. Thus, it is no surprise that most churchmen have favored a regular provision through which a reasonable number of refugees could be received by this country annually. The need is a constant and pressing one; there is always revolution somewhere in the world, always a flood or famine some place, always a dam breaking, always an earthquake. There are always people who face disaster or oppression, who are desperate and need to leave their homeland and start life over again with courage and hope. American Christians have wanted their own country to represent such a haven, and further, they have demonstrated their support for such a provision by sponsorship of thousands of displaced persons and Hungarian and Cuban refugees.

Racial discrimination as embodied by the Asia-Pacific Triangle has represented a particularly intolerable indecency to the Christian conscience. Many Christian leaders have been in the forefront of the civil rights struggle at home and they feel that prejudice, a denial of the dignity of man, must be rooted out of all national policies whether domestic or foreign. The church, universal in concept, has often been handicapped in its missionary efforts by foreign policies that are an embarrassment to the gospel it proclaims.

The national origins quota system, enacted largely in its present form in 1924, was established in part because of post war isolationism, because Anglo-Saxon and Teutonic peoples were felt to be a "superior breed," and because it was believed that citizens of certain nations were less law-abiding than others. Today rational persons no longer find these reasons tenable and are more inclined to have a man judged by his individual character, health, intelligence, and skills rather than on the basis of his national origin.

Will the legislation now being considered meet the requirements for adequate reform of our immigration laws? It appears that the Administration-sponsored bill (S. 500 and H.R. 2580) would make the fundamental changes needed to answer the needs of those desiring to emigrate, to strengthen our foreign policy abroad and provide skilled workers in short supply at home.

. . .

Citizens who wish to register their convictions on immigration legislation are encouraged to do so now. Favorable action from the respective Judiciary Committees of the House and Senate is expected soon. However, the measure could face considerable opposition on the floor. Also, one must remember that in a recent Gallup poll only 51 percent of the persons interviewed favored changing our immigration laws.

A Harris survey in May of this year seemed to indicate that Americans oppose eliminating the national origins system. Thus, without vigorous citizen support, the immigration bill could easily be defeated.

As President Johnson proclaimed eloquently in his State of the Union address: "We were never meant to be an oasis of liberty and abundance in a world-wide desert of disappointed dreams." Instead, through this legislation, Americans can share their liberty and help to actualize men's desperate dreams.

. . .

Testimony before committees of both the House and Senate was submitted recently by the Division of Peace and World Order of the Methodist Church. The Division quoted a portion from the General Conference's statement on immigration:

"Freedom to reveal and to choose one's place of residence is a basic human right and a useful outlet for tensions that develop both within and between nations. We recommend a continual re-examination of the immigration laws of the nations in light of this freedom. We condemn the provisions in such immigration laws which legalize racial and cultural discrimination and deny to persons desiring to enter a nation from other lands the respect and justice due to all men."

The Methodist testimony, after seeking to lift up and apply some general principles on the basis of the official Methodist positions, concluded by stating: "We believe this legislation to be in the best interests of the United States and that it would constitute a distinct improvement in immigration policy from the standard point of both morality and Christian compassion."

"The Siege at Wounded Knee," Lee Ranck, e/sa, 1973

Editor's Note: This is an interpretative report on the confrontation between American Indians and the federal government at Pine Ridge Reservation. Staff member Rev. John P. Adams was at one point a lead negotiator during the standoff.

The [Indian] woman huddled on a bench in one corner of the basement of Holy Cross Episcopal Church in Pine Ridge, South Dakota. She pressed a sick, gasping baby boy against her breast and watched her ten-year-old son hop off-and-on cement steps.

The woman fought to stay awake, then gently placed her baby, sucking on a near-empty bottle, on the bench and rested her head against the wall. She appeared exhausted, defeated, dispirited—one of a number of residents of Wounded Knee who fled in fear the night heavy gunfire erupted between militant Indians holding the site of the 1890 massacre and federal marshalls encircling them. The American Indian Movement (AIM) had chosen the historic place for the next of a number of demonstrations pointing up Indian grievances.

When asked how she felt about the AIM action that had made her a refugee fifteen miles from her Wounded Knee home, the woman shoved aside her exhaustion. She forced husky words across strained vocal cords while her dark eyes flashed anger, determination, and defiance.

"If there is no agreement by 2:00 o'clock this afternoon, I'm walking back in there with my boys. If the marshalls want to put a bullet in my back, let them. We're going home.

"AIM is pointing up the problems. We're deprived of our rights. The government has made slaves out of us . . . the first Americans. But AIM isn't acting for itself or for me. They doing this for the kids."

The Oglala Sioux Indian mother looked lovingly at her two boys. "Maybe someday," she began, then broke off as her voice choked up and her face trembled. Soon she began again, determined to let this white man know her feelings.

"I hope to raise another Russell Means (one of the leaders of the AIM group holding Wounded Knee) to speak up for our people. This was our country first. I am going to teach my boys how to speak up . . . to go out and get what is theirs, no beggaring around. And I believe God will help them."

At 1:45 p.m. the woman picked up her baby boy, took her ten-year-old son by the hand, left the Episcopal basement and headed out the road toward Wounded Knee.

Roadblocks on Bigfoot Trail

If the woman pressed her resolution to go home to the besieged hamlet nestled between rolling South Dakota hills, she ran into problems. If she followed Route 18 out of Pine Ridge, then walked left on Bigfoot Trail, named for the chief who died in the Wounded Knee slaughter, she encountered the FBI roadblock several miles from her home. Agents with high-powered rifles at-the-ready turned her back. A quarter of a mile down the road heavily armed US marshalls manned a second roadblock, and a half-mile further the Indians had built their own roadblock with the hulks of burned cars.

The government forces had set up similar blockades on the roads from Porcupine and Manderson, in fact on every artery into Wounded Knee. Federal automobiles or, more ominously, Armored Personnel Carriers (APC's) blocked the roads and marshalls patrolled the hills. Nobody (without proper credentials or clearance) was getting in or out of Wounded Knee (though some AIM supporters sneaked past the agents at night to enter and exit the area).

The incident at Wounded Knee presented an almost unreal sensation, a historical drama with different players and a somewhat different scenario, yet also the same—the several hundred Indians in the gully entrapped by troops on the surrounding hills. Could it be a potential rerun of the event some eighty-odd years ago when an estimated 300 Indians died under the guns of the US Cavalry?

"This is war," one observer declared. He was right in that the elements to carry on war were present, and periodically used—bunkers and tracer bullets and flares, war paint and war planes. When would the bugle sound and the troops come charging down the ridges (riding APC's instead of horses) to obliterate the puny opposing forces?

That could not happen, of course, because the Indians who had precipitated the drama by taking over the Wounded Knee community had chosen well. Surely the government would not or could not allow another massacre at Wounded Knee, no matter what the provocation. (But how much law-breaking, no matter what the motivation, can a government tolerate?) The drama, sketched daily in the national media, had already stirred repercussions from Indians across the country, and bloodshed would certainly incite many more disruptive red power demonstrations. (Those demonstrations will inevitably come anyway since the cry of "red power" for Indians, like "black power" for blacks, has grown from a whisper to a shout.)

The American Indian Movement has been in the forefront of the upsurge in Indian militancy. Begun in Minneapolis in 1968, AIM was described by one of its leaders as "merely a group of Indian people who choose to band together to improve the conditions in society in which Indian people have to live." AIM leaders have rejected the idea that this country has an "Indian problem." Instead they call it a "white man's problem." They angrily point to discrimination and inaction (and some 380 broken treaties) which have produced Indian high school drop-out rates of 64–90 per cent, alcoholism, high suicide rates, infant mortality three times greater than the national average, a life span in the forties, and an average annual income far below the poverty line.

Steadily AIM has gained in strength and militancy since its beginnings. Its leadership during the occupation and devastation of the Bureau of Indian Affairs building in Washington, D.C., last November brought new fame—or notoriety, depending on the viewpoint. But AIM got some results with that militant and costly action and it got a lot of publicity for the suppressed and long suffering minority from which it has sprung. The Wounded Knee takeover will bring some of the same. It already has.

The Press Tells the Story

The press covered Wounded Knee with all the enthusiasm and technical skill it could muster for a "good story." In fact, debates have begun even within its own ranks on whether it covered Wounded Knee or really "made" some of the drama occurring there. Whatever its role in the situation, the press was very visible—parked in mobile vans across from the AIM-occupied Wounded Knee Trading Post and hovering around the BIA building in nearby Pine Ridge. The AIM leaders naturally knew how to make good use of press eagerness.

The press chronicled the AIM demands: investigation of alleged unfair treatment of the Oglala Sioux by the BIA; investigation of hundreds of treaties that the government made with the Indians, then broke frivolously, following the opportunistic theory of the white man's "manifest destiny" to rule this land; and more specifically, ouster of Richard Wilson, chairman of the Oglala Sioux tribal council, whom the militants accuse of political patronage and corruption and of being a BIA puppet.

The press portrayed, quoted, and photographed the AIM leaders: Clyde Bellecourt, Carter Camp, Dennis Banks, and Russell Means, the tall, handsome, stoic Oglala Sioux. It pointed to their criminal records, aired their rhetoric, and recorded their determination.

The press also detailed the action: periodic gunfights and minor wounds, the continuing possibility of a bloody conclusion to the incident; the ceasefire proposal, withdrawal of federal agents, and subsequent replacement of the blockades; the declaration that the Wounded Knee area had seceded from, and was at war with, the United States; the changing demands; the continuing negotiations with officials from Washington; the involvement of the National Council of Churches in negotiations and in providing food and other necessities to the AIM insurgents.

According to Richard Wilson, chairman of the Oglala Sioux Tribe and bitter opponent of AIM, the press distorted the situation at Wounded Knee by focusing on the dissidents. Clearly miffed because, in his words, "negotiations between the armed activists and the federal government were seldom cleared through the constitutionally-elected leadership of this tribe," Wilson stressed the importance of the tribal government, which, in his eyes, AIM sought to overthrow.

"As in any democratic process, the tribal government has been slow. But one must realize that tribal governments have carried the additional burden of a reluctant and paternalistic bureaucracy, years of hostile congresses, and constant threats of seizure of our lands and water rights by greedy white citizens and industries. . . . And now we are faced with fighting Indians from other parts of the country."

A Highly Complex Drama

Wilson's words emphasize part of the complex Wounded Knee situation. The unfolding drama included many players: the AIM leadership, from both outside and inside the tribe, supported by the younger more militant residents of the Pine Ridge Reservation; the Tribal Council, supported by older, more conservative residents, but considered corrupt and ineffective by the militants; the BIA with headquarters in Pine Ridge, according to militants, an ineffective bureaucracy caring for Indians in their depressed reservation existence, but also an employer of a large number of Indians; Department of Interior and Department of Justice, two segments of the government with sometimes differing, even conflicting, opinions on how to handle the dangerous situation; the reservation residents who continually live with poverty, poor medical care, paternalism, and neglect.

The National Council of Churches entered into the complicated situation in an effort to help avoid bloodshed, to serve as a "broker" or mediator in the negotiations between opposing forces, to help mitigate the human need resulting from the AIM action and the government response. The Rev. John P. Adams, primary liaison representative of the NCC at Wounded Knee, explained the NCC presence this way:

"The National Council of Churches has demonstrated that it is dedicated to non-violent and significant change, and for this reason the NCC has been present in this place. The NCC's representatives have sought to work here in ways that would help keep communications open, furnish constructive alternatives to violence, and demonstrate the common faith that ultimately all of us have in one another—if this country is to face a future filled with hope and justice."

Tribal Council President Wilson did not welcome the NCC involvement and, in fact, described it as an encroachment on the Oglala Sioux Tribe. He worked hard to still the NCC operation and finally did obtain a court order that resulted in a March 18 removal of all supporting staff for the NCC liaison representative. A week later the same court order was served on Mr. Adams, who moved across the nearby border into Nebraska to continue his efforts by phone. Court action was initiated to attempt to get the removal order rescinded, since both AIM and government negotiators wanted Adams to continue on the scene.

"The National Council of Churches negotiation team never once bothered to clear their activities with the Tribal Council or the tribal chairman," Wilson heatedly declared. "We Indians must be reminded that unsolicited interference by the organized church in Indian Affairs throughout history has always resulted in the loss of Indian lands, Indian rights, and Indian lives."

He had a point, one repeatedly pointed up by author Dee Brown in his best-selling *Bury My Heart at Wounded Knee*. Throughout the frontier history, clergymen, presumably interested in Christianizing the Indians, did regularly turn up to help bilk Indians of their land or convince them of the worth of treaties, which were regularly negated at the whimsey of the white man. A young public health doctor in the hospital standing on a hill overlooking Pine Ridge stated the fact in a softer, but just as poignant, manner: "The Indians have listened to too many church people who have said they would do something for them and then messed up their lives."

Wounded Knee Brings Church Division

Such attitudes or comments appeared somewhat irrelevant to the NCC operation at Wounded Knee. But tribal Chairman Wilson, as could be expected, opposed any action giving sustenance to the AIM forces or that sought a negotiated settlement, and the NCC effort worked at both. Thus the Episcopal complex (church, rectory, home of Sister Margaret Hawk, an Indian born on the reservation and now a Christian education worker there) has served as the NCC base tended to be an enclave surrounded by a hostile community, including its churches. The congregation of the Episcopal Church of the Holy Cross, where NCC volunteers lived and worked from the basement until ordered out of town, opposed involvement with the "outside church people." Most of its members have close ties to the BIA and support the tribal government.

"This involvement may be a disaster for this church," explained Father George Pierce, Episcopal priest in Pine Ridge and superintendent of reservation Episcopal churches. "But there was no way to avoid disaster.

The protagonists on both sides are Episcopalian, so I couldn't do right if I wanted to."

"I involved this church because I agreed with the NCC reasons for being here—to seek to avoid any loss of life on any side, to care for any people who were suffering because of this incident. Unfortunately the community cannot deal with the problems and the tribal government can't handle it because the people are divided in their support—some go with the government, others with AIM. In this situation the NCC took the initiative that was necessary."

Church representatives—from national, state, and local levels of various denominations, including United Methodist Bishop James Armstrong of the Dakotas Area, Wesley Hunter of the Association of Christian Churches, and Homer Noley of the Board of Global Ministries—did become deeply involved in the NCC program led by John Adams. Director of the Department of Law, Justice, and Community Relations of the United Methodist Board of Church and Society, Adams has in recent years earned a reputation as an expert in crisis intervention. He has honed his negotiating and mediation skills, as well as his invaluable contacts with government officials, on the multiple crises that have erupted in this volatile era—open housing demonstrations in Milwaukee, the Selma march, the Chicago conventions, D.C. Poor People's Campaign, the Black Manifesto, Kent State, Attica, and the Miami Beach conventions. In Miami, Adams was one of the organizers of Religious and Community Leaders Concerned (RCLC), which set up a network of neutral observers in an effort to help keep the peace.

The much-publicized cease-fire agreement that avoided a major confrontation at Wounded Knee on March 8 was drawn up by the NCC team and incorporated observers similar to those used by RCLC. Clergymen from nearby states and young "church movement types" from across the country made up the NCC observer corps, which moved into position for a time around Wounded Knee, then was removed when the rapidly fluctuating situation changed again.

That fifteen-point cease-fire agreement called for a "heavy" NCC role. Besides providing case-fire observers, the NCC, with other church groups, took on responsibility for supplying food and other necessities to Wounded Knee residents and to the AIM personnel. The NCC team was also assigned responsibility for negotiating a staged withdrawal of weapons by AIM and the Department of Justice forces, for helping provide legal counsel to AIM leadership charged with crimes relating to the Wounded Knee action, and for monitoring arrests, detentions, arraignments, and legal actions resulting from the Wounded Knee protest action. The agreement further indicated that the NCC would promote a national appeal for public contributions to the Wounded Knee Memorial Trust Fund of 1973 and would urge member denominations of the NCC to make funding of programs related to the problems of American Indians a top priority.

After the situation changed and federal forces again tightened the noose around Wounded Knee, the NCC team spent its energies continuing to fulfill two of the roles designated by the agreement—facilitating negotiations and providing food and other necessities. Every time a camera focused on Assistant Attorney General Harlington Wood going into Wounded Knee to negotiate, the familiar Adams face seemed to turn up. Both government officials and AIM leaders respected the key role played by the NCC negotiator, but the Tribal Council decried the activity.

While the negotiations continued, The NCC also delivered food, medical supplies, and other necessities into the blocked off hamlet; it was, in fact, the only group allowed to enter with the life sustaining supplies. Drawing on some $6000 provided by various denominations, the NCC team bought the food and supplies from local stores, piled them in the Episcopal basement, daily loaded them into its vehicles under supervision of a US marshall, and drove the materials into Wounded Knee with a[n] escort from the Community Relations Service of the Department of Justice. Furthermore, the NCC handled coordination at Wounded Knee of the efforts of the National Wounded Knee Medical Relief Team, established by the Medical Committee for Human Tights to provide medical care for all members of the Wounded Knee community for as long as necessary.

A Pine Ridge Reservation Human Disaster Fund, established by religious groups, including the NCC, provided a mechanism for persons across the nation to contribute food, clothing, blankets, medical services, and other essentials during the emergency. Father Pierce chaired the fund committee and Sister Hawk administered it. Any money remaining after meeting emergency needs will go into the Wounded Knee Memorial Trust Fund. (Anyone doubting that donated funds have gone and will go for a good cause ought to spend some time on the reservation.)

"The National Council of Churches' representatives have become even more clearly aware of the suffering to which the American Indian has been subjected since the white man came to this continent," John Adams reported from Pine Ridge. "The United States government has, in previous administrations over a long past, made agreements that purported to guarantee benefits and rights to the Indians in perpetuity."

"The government has not kept many of these agreements, signed as official treaties by authorized representatives of the United States. The broken promises have caused broken lives. Agreements not kept have robbed many peoples of their cultures, their identity's, and their securities."

Good Cause for Indian Bitterness

As this comment suggests, American Indians have good cause for bitterness that erupts into militant actions. Unfortunately, little progress generally occurs on any social problems until extreme acts or the terrible results of inaction emphasize the problem.

Everyone involved with Wounded Knee admitted that the AIM action had at least one positive aspect. It drew attention to the problems and desperate needs. Even Tribal President Wilson stated begrudgingly that "this incident has brought to the American public the deplorable conditions under which our people must live."

Up in the Pine Ridge Hospital public service Doctor Notevoom also recognized the attention the AIM action brought, but he lamented: "Why don't our continuing needs get some of this attention?" He pointed specifically to a shortage of 13 doctor positions, the possibility of a closed reservation hospital, inadequate medical facilities and supplies.

Even a brief stay on the Pine Ridge Reservation, and a few conversations with persons living and working there, makes one quickly aware of the underlying problems that have precipitated actions such as those taken by AIM. The problems seem legion: inadequate medical services, inadequate housing, a welfare attitude perpetuated by reservation life, poor educational facilities, bad work habits, no commercial industry to provide employment, 70 per cent unemployment or underemployment for the Oglala Sioux, white-owned cattle grazing on reservation land, programs that seem to aim at keeping the Indians on a substance level, per capita income below $1000 a year, too little federal money, a large number of reservation jobs related to the chopped OEO program, grinding poverty, religion that has little to do with life here and now.

Such problems, apparent on the Pine Ridge Reservation, are too often the typical plight of the American Indian all over this nation. Add to the social injustices an ingrained, rancid white racism that somewhere down deep inside really does hold to the inhuman American aphorism, which grew from a comment of General Philip Sheridan, that "the only good Indian is a dead Indian," and the burning fuse for repeated dramas such as Wounded Knee becomes more visible.

"Those drunken Indians out there breaking the law," a member of an eastern church school class intoned. "Are we out there to support them?" (Strict rules against alcohol and drugs were, incidentally, enforced by the AIM leadership in Wounded Knee.)

"Are you people going out there to help those kooks holdout longer," a fellow traveler in a mid-western air terminal asked. And this bitter comment from a cab driver in Rapid City, S.D., who lamented the loss of this year's tourist trade because of fear of the militant Indian.

"One federal marshall told me, 'If you have to shoot one, do it and go out and throw a brick through a window to make it look like he was breaking in,' My God, I hate them bastards. If one of them harms my wife, I'll get my shotgun and kill all I can until they get me. Just get 200 of us white people out there to Wounded Knee and let the marshalls turn their backs and we'd take care of the problem in a hurry."

But the Wounded Knee problem, and the anguish it symbolizes, cannot be taken care of in a hurry. At this writing the drama continues. The outcome, the ending, holds great import for the American Indian's continuing struggle for human dignity and equality. But no one needs to know the ending of this one specific incident (and more will follow) to understand that it, with whatever conclusion, dramatizes a massive wrong performed upon red native Americans by the swarms of white people that overwhelmed the Indians. They came piously preaching the concept that whites are destined to rule all America, invaded the Indians' land, took it from them, murdered those who resisted, and dehumanized the rest. The strong (in numbers and military technology) again prevailed over the weak.

Whatever the complexities of the Wounded Knee drama—and the history that never should have occurred but now cannot be undone which Wounded Knee represents—one fact overrides the others. We are reaping the harvest planted with horrible acts against native Americans a century ago. We are simply seeing the truth in the prophetic words of Indian peace commissioner John Sanborn, written in 1866 as he viewed the US Cavalry's expeditions against the Cheyennes:

"For a mighty nation like us to be carrying on a war with a few straggling nomads, under such circumstances, is a spectacle most humiliating, an injustice paralleled, a national crime most revolting, that must sooner or later, bring down upon us or our posterity the judgement of Heaven."[1]

"Freedom of Personhood: For All Persons," Rev. Leontine Kelly, *e/sa*, 1975

Editor's Note: The following essay is a reflection on the distinct challenges of being a black woman; Rev. Kelly was elected a bishop of the church in 1984, and became the first African American woman bishop of the denomination.

---

1. Brown, Dee, *Bury My Heart at Wounded Knee* (New York: Holt, Rinehart & Winston, 1970), 152–53.

It is a great thing to see women moving out of the kind of binding situation in which society has placed them. The new freedom women are experiencing is good, and many more women are becoming more conscious of their situation. As a black woman, my perspective of the women's movement is perhaps a little different. I am very concerned that many women in the movement seem to equate their position with that of the black minority. To me this is not a true assessment.

Some of the tactics coming out of the two movements are similar, and there has been more understanding of the black situation as women have looked at themselves. On the other hand, the white woman has been very much a part of the kind of oppression that black people, particularly domestics, have suffered. It's ironic that many women involved in the women's movement have black maids at home. Still underpaid, they are often not really thought of as persons, at the same time they seek their freedom. As women are liberated and are able to set their sights much higher than their culture or society has set them, they will become the leaders, particularly in the areas of human rights and freedom, not only because of their own situation, but because women have an innate compassion.

I am very comfortable myself as a woman, and I believe that we have some real special feelings. It is very important for women to know the kind of freedom they can experience, because then they will be more willing for men to be men, not in a muscular sense, but in terms of being whole persons, free to express compassion, understanding, and inner feelings—attributes primary to personhood.

While I see the whole movement as a freeing one for all persons, my priority as a black woman still lies with freedom for black people. As a black person I am very supportive of the black male. The situation of a black male is completely different from that of the white male. The black woman has traditionally had a freedom in society that has not been available to the male. Black society has been a matriarchal structure, stemming from slavery. There was domestic work available for women when there was no work for men. A black man needed to find whatever confidence he could within the home, since he had no opportunity to be "top dog" outside the home. A black woman was put in a position of trying to provide for the home, while at the same time trying to lend some worth and value to her husband and children in a society that said they had no value. As a black-woman, and as a minister, my concern is to build confidence in black men—to help them see themselves as persons of worth. I cannot be destructive of any move that a black male might make that would improve his self-image.

No Opportunity for Leadership

In lower income, rural areas, black males have never had any opportunity for leadership. The image of the black male has been so derogatory that very often he sees himself as no more than a person who finds his real sense of security in the corner bar, or in the little shack, where he can work out all his problems with a bottle. We need to help the black man escape that kind of fantasy existence, to come out of that weekend kind of fellowship into a community that has never felt he was a part of it. He needs to realize the opportunity and the responsibility to learn, and then to transfer that learning directly into the community to answer some of his own needs—social and economic. I see myself as part of this. I find it difficult to be "picky" in terms of nouns and pronouns, because the issues for me are greater than that. I am in the business of making people see that in Christ they are free.

Unless the free white woman really sees freeness of personhood for everyone as important, black people will continue to suffer a great deal. But I would not want to hold back on the woman's movement because of this. We have to carry on; everything has to go together; you can't hold back one for the other. Women have to see that they are a part of the changing of the total society.

Misunderstandings

One of the misunderstandings of the women's movement, I think, is the idea, held by some that if you are in favor of the women's movement, you are in fact a man-hater. That is tantamount to saying that if you work for civil rights, you are a communist. This kind of generalization is indicative of the kind of box some women are in. They have failed to recognize that they are free to move out. This is not the same as saying a woman has a right to stay home if she wants to; every woman has a right to choose what she wishes to do. The movement is not to move women out of whatever they want to do, but to free them to do and to be.

If women use their freedom to oppress people, their freedom is to no avail. If women do not see themselves as part of a movement of freedom in the world, their struggle is futile. If freeing white women is just going to mean more free white people to oppress minorities, what use is it?

Leaders of the Church

Women, particularly church women, are really fertile ground for all kinds of exposure, for all kinds of team situations, across racial and cultural lines. They need to see this as a part of their own situation. The more experiences they can have with other people, the greater their opportunity to make strides in human relations. Women have the validity, the structure, and the commitment to accomplish this if they just will. I believe the church is the area in which a woman has the most freedom. She may not hold all of the offices, but she still runs the church. The leadership may visibly be male, but the movement of the church is by women. As they move themselves within the church situation, they have the ability to move the church toward the freedom of all people.

Jesus accepted people across racial, cultural, and sexual lines. If Jesus was God revealing himself to us in human form and showing us who we are, that is how we know our importance.

"A Pillar of Fire Gave Them Light," Jane Hull Harvey, *e/sa*, 1981

Editor's Note: This is a reflection on a prayer vigil and march for the Equal Rights Amendment.

They came, 2,000 of them, from across the nation to commit themselves anew to the struggle for equality for women. The New York Avenue Presbyterian Church in Washington, D.C. overflowed with singing, pageantry and prayers as they gathered for the National Prayer Vigil for the Equal Rights Amendment on June 30, 1981, sponsored by the Religious Committee for the ERA (RCERA).

Shirley Long, life-time United Methodist, came although she had been forcefully cautioned by her supervisor not to participate because the Hatch Act prevented "partisan political activity." Shirley, for twenty years an employee of the Naval Research Laboratory, was not dissuaded because she knew that the ERA was not partisan politics, and she brought her youngest daughter, Dee Dee, sixteen years old. A member of Indian Head United Methodist Church in Maryland, she had the support of her husband and four other daughters as well.

Lillian Peel, seventy-three years old and a Disciples of Christ member, who has worked in the ecumenical movement throughout her life, traveled by bus from Williamston, North Carolina, as she had come for all the other ERA and civil rights events. Just twelve years old when women won the right to vote and sixteen when the Equal Rights Amendment was first introduced in Congress, she has vowed to work for the ERA until it is passed. "My two daughters should have received it as their birthright," she declared. "I will not die until ERA is passed."

Mamie Williams, Black pastor of Calvary United Methodist Church in Washington, D.C., came as one of the twenty-six religious leaders representing forty religious bodies (including Protestants, Catholics, and Jews) which make up the membership of RCERA. She spoke with the other voices of liberation about the commitment of the United Methodist Church to the rights of women. Reading from a statement of the 1980 General Conference of the United Methodist Church, she said:

"The gospel makes it clear that Jesus regarded women and men as being of equal worth. Nowhere is it recorded that Jesus treated women in a different manner than he did men. . . . The support of the United Methodist Church for the Equal Rights Amendment derives from a historical concern for justice, human dignity and equality for every person. . . . A constitutional amendment will insure that men and women have the same rights and responsibilities under the law."

Father Neil Mccaulley, President of the National Federation of Priests' Councils, which recently endorsed support of the ERA, came from Chicago as a friend of women and a strong advocate of their rights.

"I think it is important at this moment in history," he said, "to have strong voices in the religious community speaking out for equality for women. After Vatican II, we in the Catholic Community have been trying to read the signs of the times and those signs are certainly support of women's rights. There is a strong pro-ERA and pro-women rights movement in the Catholic community."

Rabbi Mindy Avra Portnoy came from the B'Nai B'Rith Foundation at the American University. In her homily she said: "After leaving Egypt and wandering in the desert, we arrived at Sinai to receive the Ten Commandments. We Jews have always been wary of vague promises and soothing words; we prefer our rights to be written down, etched in stone, carved in the granite of law and precedent. So too, we American women know that until our rights are printed in the text of the Constitution, we will be dependent on the whims and stereotypes of still-all-male Supreme Courts and mostly-all-male legislatures. We cannot wait another generation; we have waited 205 years too long already."

Sonia Johnson came as an ex-communicated woman whose own church had voted for her expulsion because she supported the Equal Rights Amendment. Mother of four children, she invoked the spirits of our foremothers: "Susan B. Anthony once said to a group of young women, 'Why don't you protest? When I am dead under the sod and when my ashes are floating in the air over this land, am I going to have to come back and stir you up? Why aren't you all on fire?'"

She continued: "I invoke Susan B. Anthony all the time because I think it is legitimate and appropriate to invoke all good souls. I say, 'Susan, Elizabeth, Sojourner, Alice, you great liberty loving women, come to us now. Come stir us up. Help us be as you were—all on fire."

Long Line of Witnesses

Those who came to Washington on June 30, 1981 were reminded often of the long line of faithful witnesses in the struggle for women's rights, including those who fought so bravely in winning the right of women to vote. One of that earlier generation, Alice Paul, a devout Quaker, had written the first Equal Rights Amendment in 1923, after a meeting of the National Women's Party which she had founded. At this meeting to plan for the future after the hard-won victory on the vote, it was felt that the struggle for equality for women had just begun not only in this country, but around the world.

Alice, a small, reserved woman of enormous energy, had with her followers picketed the White House, been arrested, gone to prison, and braved starvation in hunger strikes and forced feedings in order to gain that victory. Then, less than two years later, she penned a Declaration of Principles, passed by her party, that included a section stating "that women shall no longer be barred from the priesthood or ministry or any other position of priority in the church, but equally with men shall participate in ecclesiastical offices and social dignities."

A year later, Alice Paul wrote the simple and direct Equal Rights Amendment to the Constitution. She had it introduced in Congress in 1923 and for forty-nine years following.

Persons of faith have been diligent in support of equality for all persons. The Equal Rights Amendment has been supported by most major Protestant, Catholic, and Jewish bodies. Today it is still a religious issue.

In the Genesis narrative of creation, both women and men are made in God's image. This is the basis on which our Judeo-Christian understanding of equality lies. The Covenant included all people, and their covenant was not for themselves alone, but for the generations to come. The stories of women in the Old Testament are moving chronicles of strong, determined, committed women struggling along with men for liberation—Sarah, Ruth, Esther, Deborah!

However, no more moving story is being told than that of the young woman, Miriam, the sister of Moses. Her cleverness as a child was responsible for saving Moses' life and for his royal rearing in Pharaoh's court. The Song of Miriam (Exodus 15:20-21) in which Miriam led the elites on their journey out of Egypt with the music of her timbrel is perhaps the oldest bit of poetry in the Bible.

The Pillar of Fire

Using the story of Exodus with its symbols of strength and liberation, Louise Bowman, national chair of RCERA declared about the National Prayer Vigil: "Our symbol is the pillar of fire. During the Exodus, when the people were lost, regretful of having left Egypt and fearful of dying in the wilderness, the pillar of fire strengthened their will to press on to liberation."

The Rev. Delores Moss, National Coordinator of the RCERA and herself an ordained United Methodist minister, picked up on this theme:

"RCERA chose the pillar of fire because people now need powerful symbols to unite and strengthen them so that they can carry on in spite of the odds. We will continue to forge ahead for justice and equality just as our forebearers have."

At the close of the service, vigilers proceeded from the church led by a modern-day Miriam playing her timbrel. In candlelight procession, symbolizing the pillar of fire, they marched under the tri-colored banners of each of the forty faith groups of RCERA for a silent vigil at the White House. The words of Rabbi Portnoy, spoken at the service just moments before echoed through the stillness:

"As our candles flicker tonight outside the gates of the White House, let us . . . remember and declare the promise that a God of freedom and justice spoke to our ancestors thousands of years ago:

"Proclaim liberty throughout the land, unto all its inhabitants thereof."

"Journey on the Underground Railroad," America Sosa as told to Helen K. Chang, e/sa, 1986

Editor's Note: This account of being an undocumented immigrant in the United States outlines how the church as part of the Sanctuary Movement supported America Sosa on her journey.

From the article: America Sosa is not her real name. For that matter she is not really staying at Dumbarton United Methodist Church in Washington, D.C., where she has been given sanctuary. However, the hardships she endured and the dangers she faces if sent back to El Salvador are frighteningly real. With the help of her assistant and translator, Yadira Arevalo, America Sosa tells her story.

America is a very common name in Latin America. I know here it's not used at all for people; but in Latin America it's like Jane or Mary. Sosa is like Smith. So my name is Mary Smith or Jane Doe. I chose this name for one reason—because some of my family is still in El Salvador, but also because I feel I am representing the women of Central America.

You probably know that in Latin America we also think that we are Americans. The whole continent is America; the country—the United States—is called America but we are also Americans because we are on the American continent. It's not unusual for us to be using that name to call ourselves American. America is a symbolic name.

I came to the United States on March 4, 1985. I had to leave El Salvador because of the persecution I was being subjected to. It started in 1979 when the church group I worked with was being taken over by the military and they began asking for the workers of the community. I was a board member of the parish in the village of San Antonio Abad, so when the military took over they searched in the files for names of the leaders of the parish, they found my name on the list. The governmental armed forces think that leaders of the church are also political leaders. Under that belief, they persecute church workers.

As one of the leaders of the community, some of my duties included teaching catechism, giving pre-baptismal and pre-matrimonial counseling, counseling groups with marital problems and coordinating Bible study.

In January in 1979, a group made of members of the army and security forces assaulted the community retreat house, "El Despertar" (meaning "the Awakening") and assassinated on the spot, Father Octavio Ortiz Luna and four youths, aged 14 to 16 who were celebrating a spiritual retreat.

After that, the village was occupied by the military and some of the leaders and members of the Christian community, including my oldest children and I, were sought by the authorities. We moved to another place in order to protect ourselves from being arrested or killed. I thought I was safe. Then in December of 1980 one of my sons, Juan, was captured. For three days he was what we call in Latin America "disappeared," because the National Police denied his arrest.

My son was 14 years old. He was in eighth grade and was a volunteer for the Green Cross. He was detained incommunicado for three months in the National Police headquarters where he was frequently tortured, beaten and insulted. He was forced to sign an extrajudicial statement which he was not allowed to read and which claimed that he was guilty of murdering a colonel and burning some buses. Without any trial, without investigation, without the right of an attorney, he was sent to Santa Tecla prison as a political prisoner.

Seven months later he was released. Immediately afterward, my son sought refuge in the Mexican embassy because he was afraid he would be assassinated, as had happened in many other cases. The Mexican authorities granted him political asylum and he is currently in Mexico, but I haven't seen him in four years. I'm very concerned now because I don't know anything about him since the earthquake in Mexico City.

When I was searching for my son in the hospital, in the jails, in the streets, in those times of pain and frustration, I came to Comadres, the Committee of Mothers and Relatives of Political Prisoners, Disappeared, and Assassinated. They provided me with information and legal and financial assistance; but the most precious thing I found there was the moral support and human solidarity that all of the mothers offered me. They understood very well my anguish, since the same experience had already happened to them.

My Husband Beaten and Tortured

In November of 1981, three months after my son was released from prison, my husband Joaquin was arrested by the Treasury Police as he was returning from work. My husband was 49 years old, and he was a construction worker. He never worked in political issues or organizations since he was afraid to get involved. His only object in life was to work and to assure the well-being of his family.

Again I had to relive the anguish of the disappearance of one of my loved ones. In all the places where we sought my husband, they told us they had never seen him, that they didn't know him. One week after his arrest and disappearance, my husband sent us a message through a prisoner who had just been released saying that he was detained in Sotanos (secret prison) of the Treasury Police.

After many petitions and pleadings to the director of the security forces, my husband was released. The day he left prison he could not walk and had to be carried. He had been savagely beaten and tortured. The director of the Treasury Police said it had been a mistake; he said that they had confused him with another suspect.

We took him immediately to a hospital. There he received physical and psychiatric treatment because some of the beatings had been to the head and he had partially lost his memory. But it was useless. There had been internal injuries to his vital organs, and in his weakened state he was unable to withstand the potent drugs they gave him. After 15 days he died.

Because of these injustices my family has suffered, I became a member of this committee of mothers and began working with them. Finally because of my activities with Comadres, I was being searched for and persecuted to the point that I had to move almost every two or three months from one neighborhood to another to avoid capture. It became impossible to continue in that situation so I had to leave. I didn't want to leave my country, so that's why I didn't come to the United States earlier. It was a last resort; and that's when I looked for sanctuary.

I Was Offered Sanctuary

Through the help of the representative of Comadres in El Salvador, Mexico City, and at the US-Mexican border, I was able to get in contact with people that eventually helped me to cross the border. At the moment when I came into the country, the church was about to declare sanctuary. The people I got in contact with in Texas and New Mexico were members and part of the sanctuary movement. Through them I got in contact with this church (Dumbarton UMC) and I was offered sanctuary.

Leaving El Salvador was not that much of a problem. I got a visa to arrive legally in Mexico City, then I took an airplane to the US-Mexican border. The problem began there at the border.

Immediately after I arrived at the airport the immigration police and agents in Mexico took my passport and all my money. The woman who was waiting for me, who is actually a member of Comadres in Mexico, convinced the immigration police that I was only coming to her house. Finally they agreed to let me leave, but without my documents. If I wouldn't leave my documents there, they would have returned me to El Salvador.

I stayed in the house of this woman until there was a good possibility of crossing the border into the United States. Finally the day came and I crossed the river—the Rio Grande. It was 11:00 pm and on the other side of the border—that means El Paso—there were people waiting for me. They were members of the sanctuary movement. So I walked across. The river wasn't too deep, about as high as my hip. If I had been caught by the police then, I would have been arrested and returned to El Salvador.

There, people who were waiting on the US side took me to Albuquerque, New Mexico; then they bought my airline ticket and I came here to Washington, D.C.

A Protection for Me

Some people have the image of sanctuary that the refugee stays in the church all the time and does not leave to go any place. But for me sanctuary means more the support of that church community rather than the building. Sanctuary is a protection for me. It is a way to be supported by church people. Also it is a way to survive because the church is taking care of my economic needs.

Because I travel around to speak out and spread the message about what's going on in El Salvador, I am vulnerable. There is the possibility that I may be arrested in an airport when I go to New York or Los Angeles or whatever. At any time, if the INS comes here and finds me and they're looking for me specifically, they will arrest me. But I'm not suffering a kind of selective persecution from the INS. I am very much aware of the danger but I haven't felt really threatened. If I start thinking about it too much, I will get a psychosis of persecution and I won't be able to do my job here—and that is to spread the message about what's going on in El Salvador.

A Threat for the Family

If I am sent back to El Salvador I may be captured and later on assassinated or maybe become disappeared. Five of my seven children are still in El Salvador and I don't know what can happen to them because one never knows what can happen to a person who is at the hands of the governmental forces. They could be in danger because they are my children and because I am a member of Comadres. Members of Comadres—even though this is a humanitarian group— have received a lot of persecution from the government. They could be in danger also because my son, Joaquin, who is a worker in the non-governmental human rights commission, is being unjustly accused of being a member of a guerrilla organization. And that means a threat for all the family.

There is a special persecution against people or institutions that are protesting human rights abuses. Four members of that non-governmental commission where my son worked have been killed already. And two of the members were captured and later on became disappeared. The rest of the founders and former co-workers are exiled. That's why in 1983 new members came to the commission—because all the old founders and workers had already been killed or disappeared or were in exile at that time.

It's very difficult to be in El Salvador right now because even though you may not have a political link with the insurgents or whatever forces, everyone who protests against injustices or violations of human rights is in danger. What the North American people can do to help is provide us with the moral and economic support so we can continue with the work here in the United States and also with Comadres in El Salvador. We ask for your solidarity in order to help free people who have been captured.

My plans here in the United States are basically to educate people about the situation in El Salvador and also talk about the organization I represent which is Comadres. Our message is of peace and justice. That's why we are supporting a political solution to the conflict in El Salvador.

Only when there is justice in El Salvador; only when there is a government—a true, democratic government—that would respect democracy and human rights, only then will all of this persecution end. When this happens, I will definitely return to El Salvador.

"Johnny Imani Harris: Dignity for Death Row," Margy Stewart, e/sa, 1987

Editor's Note: The church's attention to mass incarceration and capital punishment is exemplified in the following article.

From the publication: Stewart was chairperson of the Church and Society Committee, Hanover United Methodist Church, Hanover, Indiana. She interviewed Johnny Imani Harris in Alabama's Holman's Prison. In its March 1987 meeting, the General Board of Church and Society voted to support and join efforts by other groups and organizations seeking the commutation of Harris' sentence, to send a letter of support to Harris and his legal counsel, and to authorize the Board's president tand general secretary to join in any amicus brief filed in support of commutation of Harris' sentence.

Johnny Imani Harris is a tall, attractive man in his early forties with salt and pepper hair and a kind smile. According to Alabama's criminal justice system, he's a rapist, robber, and murderer of a prison guard. But the National Alliance against Racist and Political Repression, other human rights groups, and Harris himself have labored for many years to expose that image as a false one. They show the world a different Johnny Harris—an innocent Black man mauled by class and racial discrimination. Their efforts were recently strengthened by the General Board of Church and Society of the United Methodist Church, which, at its March 1987 meeting, agreed to file a "friend of the court" brief on Harris' behalf.

These groups tell how the Ku Klux Klan and police harassed Harris and his family in 1970 when they moved into an all-white Birmingham neighborhood. They say that Harris' apathetic court-appointed attorneys never gave him an opportunity to prove his innocence of rape and robbery charges—charges that may well have been trumped up as an extension of the harassment campaign. Indeed the lawyer on the rape charge (then a capital crime) never even visited Harris between the arraignment and the trial; Harris was forced to accept a life sentence to avoid the electric chair.

Harris' supporters further contend that following a rebellion against atrocious prison conditions, Harris, then an outspoken advocate of prisoner's rights, was made a scape-goat and used by Attorney General Bill Baxley to bring the death penalty back to Alabama. They point to the unfairness of Harris' trials before all-white, rural juries and to the discriminatory nature of the death penalty in general, used overwhelmingly against minorities and the poor. They continue to build a national and international movement for Harris' freedom and to pursue remedies in the courts, with some recent success as the Supreme Court in June struck down a statute similar to the one under which Harris was convicted. Alabama, however, continues to keep Harris on death row.

As Harris and I settled in to chat in the uncomfortably warm and noisy visitor's room of Alabama's Holman maximum security prison, the man who struck me from the first as charming and gracious (in a way that many Southerners are charming and gracious) soon came to impress me also as an unusually empathetic individual. No matter what we talked about—South Africa, family, art, prisons, white poverty, racism—there seemed to be an understanding of the situation of others and a wellspring of good will for them underlying all his words. The development of empathy is not something greatly encouraged by our society in general, let alone by the most brutal of all its institutions. Therefore, my overriding question to Harris soon became how he could stay open to people after all that he had suffered at others' hands.

Strength from Ties with Others

Harris thought for a moment and then told me that he believed that strength and callousness were two different things. "My strength has come from ties with others—from unity and solidarity, from the God-given understanding we were meant to share," he said. "Without that, I wouldn't have made it. There are people who cave in mentally, who give in to the abuse and the confinement. I'm trying not to let that happen to me."

Harris hasn't always been able to rise above the brutality of the system the way he does today. "Do you know, I used to be kind of terrible?" he said. When he first came to prison, he told me, he was defensive, angry, and easily provoked. He thought only about his own wrongs. "If I got $10 from home, I spent $10 on myself," he said.

Prison conditions at that time were so abusive that a federal judge later declared them to be "cruel and unusual punishment . . . barbaric and inhumane." The filth and overcrowding, the beatings and denial of medical care, all combined to proclaim convict-abuse acceptable to the state. Degraded by his environment and without apparent recourse, Harris searched for dignity within. "I always knew I could become a better person if I could put the negative aside," he said. He was aided by his family's strong religious values. His mother literally gave her life for another: she died shielding Harris' older brother from an assailant with a knife.

Another positive influence was a prisoner named Jerry White, a soft-spoken jailhouse lawyer who impressed Harris by helping fellow inmates for free—and by throwing himself into their cases as if they were his own.

White was one of several people who "stimulated the faith I already had in myself."

But the truly catalytic contact, according to Harris, came through exposure to a prisoners' rights group called Inmates for Action (IFA). In 1972, IFA staged an effective work stoppage during the sugar cane harvest on the prison farm. Though over 300 were punished in the wake of the strike, Harris was drawn to the organization.

A More Positive Way

"They showed me a more positive way, a more educational way than the way I had been active prior," he said.

"My attitude changed toward everybody. I stopped getting mad. I started thinking: even though I didn't finish high school, there was no need to cut myself off from learning, no need to stop improving myself."

Harris joined a book club and participated in discussions. He began to help others with writs and speak out against abuse.

"We tried to take a firm stand against people being beat for no reason or for the slightest reason," he said. In honor of the spiritual change he was undergoing, Harris added a new middle name—"Imani," which means "Faith" in Swahili and which he uses interchangeably with his given name.

Harris understood the administration's hostility to the IFA. "The system wanted you to be passive and submissive," he said. "Whatever they said, right or wrong, just accept it. But the IFA philosophy was: regardless of your position of confinement, you are still a human being and deserve to be treated as such. Regardless of your status, there are still some things that you are entitled to."

The administration tolerated, even at times seem to encourage ethnic animosity and inmate-on-inmate violence. But the multiracial IFA taught a different goal: "Support each other, educate each other, teach each other." And the IFA, through a sister organization, Family for Action, was a link to the outside world. "We were concerned about people being singled out," Harris said, "If we saw someone being abused, we would try to get the word to Families for Action. That was the kind of support the system didn't want us to have."

On January 18, 1974, when the prison rebellion occurred, "half of the people in segregation were there because of their disagreement with the system, not because they had violated any of the rules," Harris said. "They were outspoken, so here came the phony charges."

Harris maintains that all of the violence that occurred that day was unnecessary, from the initial beating of an inmate and the stabbing of a [hostage] guard to the shooting of inmates as the guards stormed the tier and the murder of an IFA leader as officials took him to the hospital. During the rebellion, the prisoners had just one demand, answered by gunshot: that they be allowed to tell what was happening to people from the outside world.

"That would have stopped a lot of it right there," Harris said. "The violence only creates bigger problems than had been there to begin with."

Lifer Singled Out for Prosecution

Though Harris—whose life sentence made him the only image eligible for the death penalty—was singled out for prosecution in the murder of the guard (no one was indicted in the murder of the inmate), the state did not maintain that he was the actual killer. "It is not our position that this defendant was actually holding the knife or anything else. We don't contend that this defendant stabbed the guard," said Assistant Attorney General George Van Tassel at a pre-trial hearing. Rather, Harris' participation in the IFA and in the rebellion was construed as indirect involvement in the death. Despite this fearsome construction put on his politics and the price he has had to pay, Harris refuses to dissociate himself from his stand for prisoners' rights. "Being involved in a just cause is nothing to be ashamed of," he said.

Harris has been under a sentence of death since 1975—longer than anyone else in Alabama. "You can't forget it for one moment, but you can't dwell on it every moment," he said. When new folks come, I tell them 'Long as I've been here, let me give you some advice: In spite of your situation, as terrible as it might be, pick one hour each day and think about your case. Don't think about it all day. Go on with your life, write letters, learn!'

"I have been afraid, yes, of what man might determine and do—but not of earth itself or what might follow. Life isn't complete until death steps in. But I want it to be ordained by God when I die. I don't want it to be a decision made by man."

I asked Harris if the large amount of mail he gets from supporters ever caused any problems between him and his companions on death row. He immediately shook his head. "They tease me; they don't envy me," he said. "We're like a family. We share things back and forth, help each other out. For example, the other day I didn't have any cigarettes, so I called down the row, "Hey, let me have some cigarettes, will you?' This guy answered back, 'You the only person I know writes people all over the world and runs out of cigarettes.' They tease me like that."

Harris says he will never stop fighting for his "family." He made me promise that I would ask my church to write letters for clemency for two young men on his tier whose execution dates have recently been set. "We get so involved with each other, our suggestions and ideals—we all pull together," he said.

"They're Just Going to Execute You"

Physical abuse is less now than before the rebellion, Harris told me, though it hasn't disappeared altogether. In its place, however, is a series of gratuitously sadistic administrative actions. Recently some prisoners' mail was kept from them until they went on a hunger strike, filed a court action, and generated outside support. Similarly, when Harris had pneumonia, a guard refused him his medicine, saying, "Why should the state waste good medicine on you? They're just going to execute you anyway."

"That's the sort of negative attitude we face here everyday," Harris said. "I get angry about it just like other people do. They try to get you into a war of the minds. You would have to experience it to fully understand the whys, reasons and what's during an exchange of that nature." The struggle for dignity and humanity inside the prison sometimes seems like a boxing match that never ends. No matter how many rounds you successfully survive, no matter how weary and bloody you become, you never get to take off the gloves and go home.

Through it all, Harris cherishes and nourishes the mutually supportive relationships that are his lifelines. "A sane person would go insane here without some kind of defense," he said. "Mine is communication with people. I couldn't have made it without them. Do you know where I get a lot of my strength? From a bunch of kids, all over the world. It's the things that they say, the things they want to do that gives me the courage and determination to carry on." Children have written to Harris from Israel, Sweden, Finland, West Germany, South Africa, and the U.S.S.R. One little girl wrote, "I don't think anyone has true freedom except the birds, the rainbows and the sun. But if I had the precious chance to have true freedom, I would give it to you."

After 12 years on death row—once coming within hours of execution—Harris may soon learn again what it is like to live out from under a sentence of death, due to the recently declared unconstitutionality of a statute similar to the one under which he was convicted. Harris was quick to point out, however, that most of the 2,000 others on death rows around the country have not been so lucky. Indeed, in two other recent decisions, the Supreme Court has removed obstacles to the death penalty, making widespread executions more likely.

Harris' supporters are now asking people to write to Alabama Attorney General Don Siegelman (Montgomery 36104) requesting that Harris not be retried. It is a crucial period in his case. In the next few years he could be paroled—or returned to death row.

Despite these radically different scenarios for the future, in one fundamental way Harris' plans remain the same. He said, "In no way can I individually repay every person who has been supportive and stood with me through this long ordeal. There is something I can do, however, that would make them proud to have made that effort: I can do for someone else what has been done for me. Twice charges were brought against me that were false and untrue. If it can happen to me two times in one state in 20 years, how many others must be caught in that dragnet?"

I thought about that as I drove away from Holman prison, past gangs of Black prisoners working by the road under the watchful eye of white, shotgun-toting guards. Like Johnny Harris, those prisoners have been falsely labeled all their lives because of race and poverty and they are now facing the stigma of convict status, too. I wonder what truths those false labels are concealing—about them and about the injustices still rampant in our land. And in the suppression of those truths, what gulfs between different sectors of our society have been made to widen?

Twice the State of Alabama has said that Johnny Imani Harris isn't fit to live. But the question is not only whether Alabama will now cease its persecution of Johnny Harris; the question is also whether our society itself will survive if we as a people do not learn, as he has learned, to value human relationships most of all and to struggle, as he is struggling, for dignity and justice.

"We Can't Let It Happen Again!, an interview with Aiko Herzig-Yoshinaga and Jack Herzig," Lee Ranck, *Christian Social Action*, 1989

Editor's Note: This article reflects on the actions of two United Methodists who sponsored along with others a call for the US government to formally apologize and offer redress for Japanese-American internment during World War II.

From the article: Archival Research by Aiko Herzig-Yoshinaga and Jack Herzig Uncovered Evidence that Racist Stereotypes, Not "Military Necessity," Motivated the World War II Internment of Japanese Americans.

On October 31, the US Supreme Court denied certiorari to plaintiffs in *William Hohri et al v. United States*. This action rebuffed and terminated a near-ten-year effort by a group of Japanese Americans to challenge the constitutionality of their World War II exile and internment.

"Among the issues the Court declined to consider was, the fact, established in the US Court of Appeals for the Ninth Circuit, that our wartime government had knowingly suppressed evidence in its argument before the court in Hirabayashi and Korematsu. This evidence contradicted the factual underpinnings of its allegation of military necessity and demonstrated that racial animus, not military judgement, had been its motive.

"Unlike the legislative and executive branches of government which recently agreed to provide restitution and to apologize for their wartime behavior, the Supreme Court has allowed its wartime decisions to stand—without even the courtesy of written opinion. The Court's silence sustains the principle that in times of national stress our government may ignore, by the mere allegation of military necessity, constitutional guarantees and protections."—*A statement issued by the National Council for Japanese Americans Redress (NCJAR) following the Supreme Court decision.*

The long list of Redress Legal Fund sponsors on the NCJAR stationery includes Aiko and Jack Herzig, whose archival work undergirded the campaign for redress of Japanese-Americans interned during World War II. Aiko Herzig-Yoshinaga, who as a teenager was shunted off to the internment camps that became her home for more 1,000 days, and her husband Jack, a retired military man, for years engaged in a mission to document the injustice of the internment action. . . .

Several weeks before the disheartening Supreme Court decision, Aiko and Jack Herzig traveled from their Falls Church, Virginia home to the *Christian Social Action* headquarters, next to the Supreme Court—the final focus of their intense efforts—for the following interview:

CSA: Your intense redress efforts grew out of your internment camp experience. Could you talk about that?

Aiko: I was just about to finish high school in Los Angeles when war broke out and the exclusion program of the government took place. The first camp I went to was Manzanar located in California; my parents and family were sent to another camp, Santa Anita, and then from there were transferred to a camp in Jerome, Arkansas, where my father became ill and died. When that camp was closed in 1944, because the government wanted to transfer the camp to a prisoner of war rather than a relocation camp, those Japanese-Americans remaining were moved to another camp in Rohwer, Arkansas.

I was in the camps a little more than three years. It was not a pleasant experience and was totally unjust. There were some real ironies in the government's action that deprived us of our rights. For instance, my older sister was born in Japan and was living in New York City at the time we were all sent to the camps, so she was not affected by this exclusion program. Here she was, an "enemy alien" as they used to call her, who came to visit us in the camps. Obviously, the government just didn't think this through carefully enough. I think the government officials in charge realized they had made a mistake, but it was too late to do anything about it. Later, to encourage those remaining in the camps to leave and start a home somewhere else (than the west coast), they offered $25 per person who would leave.

The Japanese-American people left in the camps in 1944–45 were naturally the elderly and the very small children. Younger folks went out to go to colleges, get jobs, establish their homes, and then eventually call their parents out of the camps. Government officials realized, I am sure, that unless they emptied out the camps as soon as possible, they would have another Native-Americans-on-reservations type of situation on their hands. One of the suggestions for expediting the return to normal living of the Japanese-Americans in the camps was to form an army unit of Japanese-American men to show how loyal they were, and that's one of the reasons the 442nd Regimental Combat Team was formed. John J. McCloy, Assistant Secretary of War, said he believed in the loyalty of these men and wanted to institute this fighting unit to show white Americans "that these people were OK." Of course, behind all of this was politics.

Jack, my husband, who has become my co-researcher, brings a whole different perspective. As a non-Japanese, a former paratrooper fighting the Japanese in the Pacific war, and a member of the military intelligence unit of the Army, he has a much more objective perspective and can also talk about the military aspects of the exclusion/detention program. He knows that there was never any need for this to have happened; there was no danger ever of any invasion of the Imperial Japanese forces.

CSA: In a recent article in *The Washington Post* you said that not only the politics, but racism was involved. Could you discuss that further?

Aiko: All of us realized from the very beginning that it was so obviously racist. To repeat what has been said so many times, we were at war not only with Imperial Japan but with Germany and Italy, and the same kind of actions were not taken against persons who had come from those lands.

As a matter of fact, on Columbus Day 1942, the government made a very big effort to let Americans know that Italian-Americans would not be subjected to the same kinds of restrictions as Japanese-Americans. While some individual Germans were picked up, they were not subject to the mass exclusion which we Japanese-Americans experienced. As soon as these restrictions began to be issued, many German and Italian aliens applied for citizenship, but Japanese and other Asians were not permitted by law to become citizens regardless of how long they had been here. Also Japanese-Americans were not treated the same way even in the armed forces. When the war started, many of our men were placed on reserve duty or their classification was changed to 4-C. Eventually these men were accepted back into combat and military intelligence.

Voting rights were another instance. Persons sent to Heart Mountain in Wyoming, for example, requested the right to vote, but the government said, "No, you're not here permanently." Since they had been removed from California, they couldn't vote there. So we were deprived of our citizenship rights in many, many areas. The political aspects of this injustice were quite evident. For example, when we dug into the materials in the archives, we found several memoranda and notes written by key government officials that clearly indicated Japanese people should not be released until after the November 1944 presidential election because Roosevelt would lose votes, especially on the west coast. There were notes to that effect by Attorney General Francis Biddle, by General George C. Marshall, by Assistant Secretary of War McCloy. It's heartbreaking to read something like that and realize that we were just pawns.

CSA: You've been involved in the long struggle for redress, and in August the President signed a reparations bill, but you have said you cannot accept the $20,000 it provides until the Supreme Court agrees to hear the Hohri case. Why?

Aiko: The compensation program does not really deal with the basic principle of this entire action. My point, and the point of William Hohri and the rest who would like to see the Supreme Court deal with this, is that Congress, through the law PLl00-383, has agreed to apologize to the people who were mistreated and to offer $20,000 to anyone eligible who will accept it. But Congress did not deal with the violations of constitutional rights. In 1943 and 1944 when the Hirabayashi and Korematsu cases came before the Supreme Court, it did not deal with all these different rights that were violated, but it did say that in times of war we sometimes have to give in to military judgment. However, there was not adequate examination of what the military had said, of the basis on which it had acted, or of the evidence the Justice Department had to declare that military necessity led to the exclusion and detention of Japanese-Americans.

Our evidence shows that the Justice Department knew the reason was not military necessity. We now want the Supreme Court to review the evidence and acknowledge that the Justice Department knew in 1943 and 1944 that what it was saying was not true. We found evidence that inside the Justice Department there was turmoil. The Solicitor General was advised of the facts. We know that the Army was saying untrue things. We have evidence that what Lt. General John L. DeWitt—Commanding General of the Western Defense Command—said in his final report was not true. "If we don't tell the Supreme Court we know this, we might be guilty of suppressing evidence," some of the Justice Department attorneys working on the Japanese-American legislation told the Solicitor General, who was arguing the case for the War Department against Korematsu. However, the Solicitor General chose to ignore that warning. So with this new information the Hirabayashi, Korematsu, and Yasui convictions were vacated in the lower court in recent years; but these cases did not reach the Supreme Court. What we want now in the class action law suit, Hohri et al. v. the United States, is for the Supreme Court to look at these facts, to agree that fraud had, indeed, been perpetrated upon the high court by the government in 1943 and 1944, and to come up with a judgment that is just.

CSA: What would that just judgment be?

Aiko: The Korematsu decision said that in times of war the government sometimes has to take actions such as that taken against Japanese-Americans. We want the Supreme Court now to say that there were many, many violations of our rights, civil and human rights, violations that were ignored, and we want the Constitution to be operative in times of war as well as in times of peace. We want the Court to review and reverse the decision of 1944 and to admit that those acts were unconstitutional. We want it to indicate that from now on it will be unconstitutional for this government ever to pick up groups of people and put them away on the basis of blue eyes, race, gender or whatever. Congress says the bill that was passed will be a deterrent, but that's not good enough because the Supreme Court has set a precedent on the law books that permits the government to remove people forcibly without due process of law.

CSA: So, in essence, the bill includes an apology and a little money for folks who will accept it. Do you have a bit of a feeling that this is kind of an apologetic buy-off?

Jack: That's exactly the truth. We've said many times that no price can be paid for the deprivation of liberty. Even to put it in dollar terms, if Aiko were to accept the $20,000 and divide it by the 1,000 days she spent in camp, that would come to $20 a day. Who could think that $20 a day could possibly compensate anybody for the pain and suffering, deprivation, hardship, sickness and death that took place as a result of the government's uncalled-for action. So the money aspect of it is just not to be considered at all?

Another aspect is that in 1942 the executive branch pushed to get the executive order signed—the War Department, the President and the Attorney General all pushed to get it signed. Then Congress passed a law making it a crime for civilians to disobey a military order. So the same institution that passed that law, after less than an hour debate in 1942, hurried to get the 1988 bill passed in the House and Senate. In effect, the Congress is making up now for the action it took in 1942, and the executive branch is doing the same thing in some feeble way. However, the Court still needs to repair its action.

CSA: If the Supreme Court action were repaired would your "mission" be complete then?

Aiko: Some of the major goals have been obtained—financial compensation, the apology—but we cannot consider this whole story completely closed—the last chapter we call it—until the Supreme Court does decide that it is illegal to do such things. It's not just for Japanese-Americans.

That is the crucial point—that government cannot abridge the rights of a helpless minority group and look away as if there were no rights to be considered. The bill itself says anybody who accepts this money will give up his or her right to sue the government. Some of us don't consider that the bill has dealt with the core of the problem. That's why we want the Court to look at it and come forth with the decision that somebody had actually committed fraud against the Supreme Court. We can't let that happen again.

Jack: There's another component of this, too. We found that, in populations other than the Japanese-American community, and indeed within some members of Japanese-American community, the facts just are not known. When we have appeared before groups of high school students where teachers have asked us to come talk to their students, we look at their text books and only a few lines about the internment of Japanese-Americans.

CSA: Do those textbooks say anything about this injustice?

Jack: No. It's just straight reporting. The full story needs to be told to all the people!

CSA: Could such detainment happen again in the United States? Today we've got an English-only movement, and various hate groups coming to the forefront again. It seems we need protection against a repeat of what happened to Japanese-Americans during World War II.

Jack: Think of what took place toward the end of the 70's and early in '80 when Iranians were demonstrating against the regime in Iran. Thousands of them would demonstrate in New York and other cities, and the average American who was watching would turn away and say, "Lock 'em all up." Many of these were Iranians who came to the United States to escape persecution.

CSA: Because of the experiences of the detainment camps, liberty is very important to you. What does the loss of liberty feel like?

Aiko: I think we all take it so much for granted. That's the thing I felt so strongly, even though I was a high school girl at the time I went to camp. Just the fact that we couldn't go to the corner drugstore and buy a malted milk or go to the movies. The fact that we were confined behind barbed wires with military police guarding us was a very devastating, depressing, shocking thing that made us realize what liberty meant. We were so busy trying to figure this out in our heads. All the little problems. Are we going to have enough hot water to wash the diapers today? The food was so terrible, the kids got sick and there weren't enough doctors and nurses to take care of us. So we were quite worried about our own survival. Even though we had a roof over our heads, the camp conditions were certainly not something anyone would choose to live under. During the early period of camp life, meetings conducted in Japanese were prohibited. That was a very difficult thing for our parents to deal with because they didn't understand English well. If there were to be meetings in Japanese, an administrative person had to be there as well as somebody to translate everything, so there was this loss of freedom of speech.

CSA: A lot of years have gone by since those camps. Isn't the passage of time a blockage to your effort?

Aiko: The legislation earmarks some funds for education and research; perhaps some of the appropriations could be used to put correct information into the schools. That's what is so important. People sometimes ask why I want to rock the boat so much. I hope those who see our action don't consider it disloyal or unpatriotic, but rather an effort to improve the country.

CSA: Was there any outcry when the relocation was taking place? Were churches saying, "This isn't right"?

Aiko: I think some churches and some church leaders did oppose it. However, churches tended to give deference to government decisions because they did not know what the military situation was. I think the churches failed a little bit in not coming out on constitutional grounds. It seems to me that they gave in to racism.

CSA: What's your message to the church?

Aiko: It comes down to accepting people for what they are; the church can educate its members on the importance of accepting people for what they are, without regard for race or color.

"A Time for the Church to Redefine a Nation," Rev. Joseph Lowery, *Christian Social Action*, 2000

Editor's Note: Rev. Lowery, a pillar of the Civil Rights Movement, offers the following message of calling on the church to be a prophetic voice calling on the nation to be redefined by an ethic of love. He names racial division, affirmative action, sexuality, and mass incarceration as critical issues to be addressed.

From the article: Rev. Lowery was the featured speaker at the General Board of Church and Society banquet held during General Conference in Cleveland. Christian Social Action *magazine presents an edited transcript of his remarks.*

I am pleased to be here. I retired from the church in 1992, and haven't been to a General Conference in a long time, so it's good to be here and see some familiar faces—bishops and pastors and potentates and ayatollahs.

I came because I couldn't say no to Church and Society. Agencies within the church like this one keep pulling and pushing the church to be headlight rather than brake light.

Let me get straight to my text.

There is a re-defining going on in this country. We're in the process of re-defining who we are as a nation. Matthew 25:31 reads "Inasmuch as you did it unto the least of these . . ." And in 1 Corinthians 12 Paul says, "Unto each of us is given a manifestation of the spirit for the common good." Church bodies all over the country, now and throughout the summer, Protestant bodies, will be assembling in conferences. The nation is in a critical state of transition.

As new century millennium observers we have witnessed the passing of more than a century; we have witnessed the passing of an era. The cold war, the anti-communist hysteria era as I call it where standards of appropriateness and excellence were measured and calculated by their relationship to anti-communist agenda. You could get away with anything as long as you said you were fighting communism.

And we did.

We neglected democratic institutions and principles, we perverted values, we ignored human rights abuses, we sacrificed ideals, we trivialized social sensitivity, we minimized the ethical and maximized the expedient, we glorified violence, we sanitized the electric chair, we demonized the saints and canonized the devil. All in the name of fighting communism.

In so doing, we have sown the wind and now we reap the whirlwind. The community of faith must provide leadership in re-defining the nation. We must not be taillights in re-defining the nation! We've experienced many shining and defining moments in our history: the Boston Tea Party organizing of the Methodist Church, the Bill of Rights, the Emancipation Proclamation child labor laws, collective bargaining laws, all defining moments for us as a nation. The Supreme Court decision of 1954, the 1964 political accommodations act, the 1965 Voting Rights Act, the Montgomery bus boycott where African Americans embraced self-determination—that was when we defined ourselves. No matter what the courts said, no matter what the state legislature said, no matter what the governor said, we weren't gonna ride on the back of the bus.

But the challenge to the community of faith today is to provide spiritual, ethical and moral leadership in the re-definition. Nobody ever in a rational context, expects the General Conference to be a defining moment for a nation. But who knows? God is not dead.

Opportunity to Be Prophetic

But whether it is a defining and shining moment or not, there is an opportunity for the General Conference to sound prophetic voices, to be courageous souls, to transmit signals, to light fires to ignite creative energy and send it loose in the society toward the right direction, to raise the right questions and join with the nation in seeking the right answers.

. . .

In the burning issues before us today, the church, the body of Christ, cannot assemble without wrestling with alternatives to violence, global economic justice, the disparities in income and the quality of life in our own country, the decadent criminal justice system, issues related to human sexuality, and the mandate for a new birth of spirituality. There are powerful forces busy in this country, engaged in the concerted struggle to redefine the nation in their own image. And if we're not careful, to redefine God in their own image. They would make God elitist, white, racially-supreme, male. They would ignore the text, "Inasmuch as you have done it unto the least of these . . . "

Prisoners, blind, frail, weak, oppressed, rejected, scorned—"inasmuch as you have ministered unto them" is God's self definition by his Son. How can they redefine Him in any other context? How long will we remain in this valley of superstition and ignorance about race? How long will we major in the minor of complexion and ethnicity? When children kill each other in schools and so many major issues remain. How long toil ye in this valley of racial foolishness? How long?

Authentic Interpretation

I'm a northerner . . . North Alabama. From Huntsville, near the Tennessee line. My mother cooked on a wood stove. I remember because I had to chop the wood and take out the ashes. Some good stuff was put together on that wood stove, I tell you. Biscuits I always remember. The thing about a wood stove is the color—the browning of the biscuits—depends on their placement in the oven. The back of the oven where the heat was intense the biscuits got brown; up in the front they hardly tanned, but they were all good! I like to think that God baked us in His oven of love. Using solar energy. Some of us He took out of the oven real quick! Hardly got brown at all, but they're done. Some a little longer, and got tanned, and they're done. Some a little longer, got chocolate, they're done. Some stayed overnight, got ebony black, but they're all done! All sweet, all luscious, all delicious, all objects of the love and creativity of God. How long will we toil in this valley of racial foolishness?

Yet in the context of race in The United Methodist Church, at higher levels we approach inclusiveness in strange ways. Although the real dilemma in The United Methodist Church was that at the same time we were pushing for integration, the larger community was pushing for self-determination. And under our definition of integration, how in the world do you achieve self-determination when you get swallowed-up in assimilation? Integration must be redefined. Integration is not the closing of black colleges, the wiping out of black churches. Authentic integration is not the systematic moving of all things black to all things white. Authentic integration is the emphatic movement of all things wrong to all things right. That's authentic integration! Institutions must be sensitive to serve all those who come . . . let them come, let them come.

In the church, we tend to think of integration as a one-way street: "Come on black folk, join this white church." Why the devil don't we think of white folk joining a black church? A newspaper asked me once, "Why is it that white folk don't join black churches?" I said, "why don't you ask the white folk?" I can give you my speculation. They come all the time. White folk love to hear black folk preach! Somebody say, "Amen!" And they love, God knows, to hear us sing! Why they don't join our churches? I'll tell you why. In my speculative prognosis, it's that white folks have difficulties accepting black leadership. And in the black church, the black preacher is the leader! Ain't no question 'bout that! Might be some debate in the white church, but not in the black church! Stewards in the white church might tell the preacher what he can or cannot preach, but ain't no black steward been born yet who has the gall to tell a black preacher what he can or cannot preach. They might mess around and talk about how long they can preach, but that's legitimate. I recently preached at a Baptist church, a white church, and asked the pastor, "How long can I preach?" He said, "You can preach as long as you want; the folk are going to leave at 12 o'clock."

Let's redefine economic justice. There's a frightening growing disparity in income in this country, between those who have less than they always need, and those who have more than they ever need. There's a study from Sweden that has concluded what is just for a CEO to earn compared to the worker. What's just? They concluded that maybe five to seven times (the worker's salary). Do you know what it is in this country? Closer to 300 times. And worse than that there is no debate about it. I have spoken to the stockholders of several large companies, where the CEO in one made $28 million while the migrant workers made $8000.

Church, why is all your energy dispersed in judgmental propositions about whether God can use some people who have different orientations sexually when there is hunger in the land, when there is misery in the land, a growing disparity between the haves and the have-nots? And you church, you sit around! How long?!

I wish I could answer "Not long." Martin [Luther King] made that speech himself in 1965, "How long?" and his answer was "not long." The question is still there; the answer we await. A study just released in New York shows the working poor are poorer comparatively then they were 10 years ago. And quality of life: 40 million people with inadequate coverage for health, people free to choose their undertaker but they can't choose their doctor. HMO director died the other day, went to heaven. He met St. Peter who said to him, "Sure, you can come in, but you can only stay three days."

Church! The challenge is to redefine the nation, to move from charity to love. Charity is alright, it gives a hungry man a fish sandwich, but love teaches him how to fish; love provides a job where he can buy good equipment to catch the best fish. Love provides health care and job benefits that give him security for the future. Love moves beyond charity. Church, how long? In the redefinition of a nation, we must move from charity to love.

And we must deal more realistically and courageously with the issue of affirmative action. Affirmative action was born in the New Testament. It wasn't born in the Nixon administration like some folks think. It may have been translated into public policy, but it was born in the New Testament. I heard Jesus when he said "The Son of Man comes to save those who are lost." He said that those who are well, they don't need a physician; it's those who are sick. Isn't that affirmative action? Didn't I hear Him say that a woman had 10 coins and lost one, and she put the nine aside and tore up the house until she found the one. Ain't that affirmative action? More than that, the good shepherd had 100 sheep. Ninety-nine had a two-car garage, health care, job security, but one little sheep—must have been a black sheep—lost out yonder in the wilderness, and Jesus said, "Wait a minute! Before I turn in for the night, I'm not going to put you out! I'm not going to subtract anything from you! I'm going to add something to your fellowship because no matter how comfortable you think you are, you can't be really comfortable as long as one of you is out yonder, excluded!"

How long? Draining energy over this sexuality thing. How dare you challenge God's power that He can't use anybody He wants to call. Who are you? Nobody in this room doesn't know darn well that God can use homosexuals in the ministry, because you've seen God use them. Don't sit up there with a question mark on your face, give me an exclamation point! What you're saying is, unless you deceive and keep it secret and lie a little bit, God can't use you. What a strange theology. It's like in the military, "Don't ask, don't tell." How stupid! If you deceive, you can be a general; if you're honest, you can't even serve.

I don't know that I'm right. I don't profess to be an absolutist. But I tell you what: if I'm wrong, if I'm going to err, I'm going to err on the side of granting all God's children the same equal rights. If I err on the side of compassion and justice and equal rights, if I err, I want God to forgive me!!

Violating the Sacredness of Life

Finally, in redefining the nation, the criminal justice system is too ignored by the church and is the least impacted aspect of our national life by social change. The 1999 criminal justice system is almost the exact replica of the 1909 criminal justice system. The difference is that the growing disproportion of black and Latino males, and now females, is the exaggerated distinction. A study just released in juvenile justice indicates where we're going. Nowhere in society is our racial disparity more pronounced and sickening than in the criminal justice system.

Violence, as a violation of a human dignity, is so devastating. The death penalty, where we're finding now some relief of conscience by changing the methodology—"we will not kill you by electric chair; we'll kill you by lethal injection—that makes us more decent?" We'll be more sanitary. You know who started the practice of lethal injections? The Nazis. Whether you shock me to death or stick me to death, I'm just as dead, and you have violated the sacredness of life just as much.

Beyond that, we send a message to our children at Columbine and Georgia and Arkansas that killing is an acceptable means of dealing with social problems. Doesn't the government do it?

When George Wallace was governor I met with him and I said, "Governor, let me talk to you for a minute as a Methodist preacher to a Methodist layman. God is going to hold you accountable. Governor, you have the platform of a governor from which to speak. There are folks out in the street who don't have your forum, but they want to identify with you, so they stalk in the darkness with lead pipes and shotguns and they kill white women on Highway 80 and preachers in Selma, downtown, by bashing their brains out. You are the inciter of that, and God will hold you accountable."

Make no mistake about it, we send a message in how we resolve our social problems by killing. It's no accident that in the criminal justice system, black and Latino youth are five times more likely to be incarcerated for the same offenses as white people, 44 percent more likely to be tried and 58 percent more likely to be sent to adult prisons. Black youth are charged with 40 percent of the drug crimes, but 63 percent of the persons tried for adult crimes with drugs are black. When white and black kids are charged for the same offenses, blacks with no prior record are six times more likely to be incarcerated than whites, and Latinos three times more likely. White kids are sent home with warnings while black and Latino kids are sent to prison.

You should be aware of what this is doing to the black community and to the Latino community, what it's doing to job opportunities, with attitudes toward society, what it's doing to society's soul. These policies ripple through all of American life.

I like Bill Clinton, but we have a problem with him on violence and the "three strikes and you're out" policy. Add to that the privatization of prisons, where profit depends on numbers. Look at what is happening in this country. Prisons for profit do not fit into the theology of the community of faith. Rehabilitation, non-existent.

Keep the Flame of Hope Burning

Let me close by saying that we must move from the back court of insidious insensitivity and insidious individualism to the front court of priorities and values that embrace the common good. We must move from the back court of profit by any means to profit-sharing by all means. We must move from the back court of political demagoguery that convinces white males that economic uncertainties are created by women's rights, civil rights, affirmative action, welfare reform. It's not true! It's that kind of mentality that gives (Atlanta Braves pitcher John) Rocker standing ovations at ball stadiums, because they say "he spoke what we feel." Oh Lord, to the front court of redefining American understanding of interdependence that shapes our destiny demands equal opportunity for all of God's children, that the road to fulfillment for any of us is the road to fulfillment for all of us.

Thank God that you're here, with a conscience, with the understanding that we are mandated to keep the flame of hope burning. We must not let the nation, we must not let our young people, lose hope.

And black people have particularly been a people of hope, even when we sang the blues. I know you don't know about the blues, but even when we sang the blues, we kept this flame of hope burning. We expressed this hope in hymns. "I'm so glad trouble doesn't last always." The slaves who couldn't see beyond the dark anything but the sunset of sadness and separation, yet deep down in his heart, he sang, "I'm so glad." And he sang, "Swing low, sweet chariot," and he sang, "Steal away to Jesus," talking about a wagon with hay on it, part of the Underground Railroad. Jesus and freedom were synonymous. Keep the flame of hope burning.

We can't do it half-heartedly. I saw a sign that said, "you may be past-due, but you're not past hope." Faith and work go together. The church must remember that. How many of you can associate Disney World without Mickey Mouse? Then how can you believe in faith without works? The Bible says faith without works is dead. Can you think of the Vatican without the Pope, or Einstein without math? Then how can you have faith without works? How can you have hope without stewardship? South Africa without Mandela, Rome without the Coliseum, Handel without the Messiah, Mehalia without "Move on Up a Little Higher?"

Then how can you think about faith and love of God without the cross? You got to be able to bear the cross in order to reap the crown. I think we got it backwards: Sunday doesn't come before Friday. It's Friday, then Sunday. Faith without works, hope without stewardship. . . . I can't think of Ray Charles without thinking of "Georgia On My Mind." I can't think of Aretha without "R-e-s-p-e-c-t." I can't think of New Orleans without Mardi Gras, Atlanta without the Olympics, Calvary without Jesus, Easter without the resurrection, the manifestation of the Holy Spirit without the common good, identifying God without hearing the words of Jesus: "Inasmuch as you did it unto the least of these, you did it unto me."

God bless you.

"The Body of Christ at the U.S.-Mexico border," Tricia Bruckbauer, *Faith in Action*, 2018

Editor's Note: The United States was struck with the horror of the US government separating children from their families and placing them in detention centers with very poor conditions. Church and Society visited with United Methodist ministires as well as detention centers to learn about the issue of migration further.

From the article: A first-hand account from GBCS director after delegation visit hosted by the Rio AC and Bishop Schnase.

Change Our Hearts, Change Our Minds

You see pictures, but nothing really prepares you for seeing it in person:

Hundreds of people in cages.

Many of them wearing bright orange t-shirts—the distinctive color of the U.S. prison system—given to them while their clothes are laundered.

Shoes laced together with aluminum foil.

A sea of silver Mylar blankets providing a constant hum of rustling.

This scene is the Ursula Border Patrol Central Processing Center.

I, along with three of the bishops who serve on the General Board of Church and Society and General Secretary Susan Henry-Crowe, was there on a trip coordinated by the Rio Texas Annual Conference and led by Bishop Robert Schnase, who pastored a church in McAllen for 20 years.

Throughout the trip, Schnase shared reflections from his life on the theme of borders. The bishop reflected one evening, "When we cross borders, we encounter people who would otherwise be strangers. We should be willing to put ourselves in situations that change our minds and change our hearts."

It is unlikely that anybody on the two-day border trip left McAllen without having an experience that changed their mind or heart.

It Is What It Is

We met at the border with the U.S. Border Patrol. Standing on U.S. soil, one just had to glance to the side to see Mexico 400 feet away across the Rio Grande. Four different officers spoke about their perspectives on the immigrants they apprehend. The officers shared about the harsh conditions the immigrants face on their journey and shared how they frequently save the lives of those who are starving or dehydrated.

After having been previously told that entrance into the Ursula Processing Center would not be permitted, Border Patrol escorted the group through the facility.

The images of fellow humans in cages elicited painful reactions from the group. Some members spoke with men, women and children through the fencing or offered short prayers of "God is with you." Others questioned the Border Patrol agents about the conditions in the center: Are the cages necessary? Are children over 10 (who are put in a separate cage from their parents) allowed to spend time with them? What mental health services are offered? Why must the lights be on 24 hours a day?

Upon our exit from the Center, the Rev. Maribel Vazquez, a pastor of two Spanish-speaking churches in the McAllen area, asked one of the agents, "How is your heart?"

His response was, "It is what it is, and we're just trying to do the best we can."

Never has there been a clearer understanding of the need for systemic change than "it is what it is."

Our Work as People of Faith

Later that day, the group met with Assistant Federal Public Defender Azalea Aleman-Bendiks, who is court-appointed to "defend the indigent." She is also United Methodist.

Aleman-Bendiks shared about her experience, from a judicial branch perspective, with the implementation and repercussions of what the Trump Administration calls a "zero-tolerance policy."

Since the U.S. Department of Justice implemented the policy earlier this year, the public defenders have represented upward of 150 individuals per day. That gives them mere minutes with each client to hear their story and prepare a defense.

Border Patrol told many immigrants who tried to cross the international bridge in McAllen and claim asylum that there was a 20-25 case limit on asylum claims each day. That is untrue and drove people to camp out at the bridge for days at a time and often forced people to cross the river, effectively placing them directly into criminal proceedings.

For the months when the administration was separating children from their parents, Aleman-Bendiks claimed that the government refused to provide a list of children who were separated. Public defenders were writing notes, such as "7-year-old son," on court documents to create even the smallest record of a child-parent relationship.

The group heard stories secondhand from the public defenders about how parents were told that their children were going to take showers or fill out paperwork, when the children were actually being relocated. Attorneys absorbed the trauma experienced by these parents and then had to turn around and defend them.

"They don't see these people as humans," Aleman-Bendiks said referring to the masterminds of these immigration policies. "That is our work as people of faith."

Restoring Human Dignity

It would have been easy to leave McAllen feeling desperate and heart-broken about the current state of affairs.

However, there exists a network of committed, faith-filled people working along the border to offer hospitality and restore dignity to migrants that inspired all on the trip.

The group visited La Posada Providencia, a crisis shelter for asylum seekers run by the Sisters of Divine Providence (and directed by a United Methodist) that helps clients make arrangements to meet family and friends in the U.S.

One nun spoke of her work at the shelter one Advent season when a man and pregnant woman knocked on the door of the shelter and asked if there was room to stay. It was a stark illustration of the sanctity of their work.

Good Neighbor Settlement House, a ministry of First United Methodist Church of Brownsville, was opening a respite center for migrants the day of the visit. They hope that Customs and Border Patrol will cooperate with them to provide services to asylum seekers released from custody.

A religious celebrity of sorts, Sister Norma Pimentel of the Missionaries of Jesus, welcomed the group into a shelter run by Catholic Charities of the Rio Grande Valley.

The shelter receives communication from Immigration and Customs Enforcement when they drop off migrants at the bus station. Pimental and her team then greet the hundreds of migrants at the bus station and bring them to the shelter for care.

A city manager once visited and asked, "Sister Norma, what exactly are you doing here?" She replied, "We are restoring human dignity."

The Body of Christ

It became very evident that many people are living along the southern U.S. border who have devoted their lives to fighting for the dignity of all people.

Ann Cass, who we met on one of the last visits of the trip, is no exception.

Cass has spent decades working to ensure the rights of farmworkers and now serves as the executive director of Proyecto Azteca, an organization working to build housing for those in the Rio Grande Valley. Because of Cass' experience, she offered the group an overview of the realities of a border wall, which she said would be a waste of money that could go toward building a public hospital.

Cass, a Catholic, shared a conversation that she had with a Jesuit about ministering with immigrants. "How do we welcome them into the body of Christ?" the Jesuit asked.

"They already are the body of Christ," Cass replied.

This trip to McAllen was a two-day reminder that the immigrants we hear about on the news every night are in our pews and behind our pulpits.

Will our mercy and justice responses reflect our understanding of the body of Christ?

"Church and Society Commemorates 30 Years of the Americans with Disabilities Act," Rev. Michelle Beadle, *Faith in Action*, 2020

Editor's Note: This article celebrates the passage of the American Disabilities Act, legislation that Church and Society supported, and the continuing efforts of fighting for the rights of persons with disabilities.

On July 26, the U.S. will commemorate an historic milestone in the advancement of human rights: the 30th anniversary of the signing of the Americans with Disabilities Act (ADA). This landmark legislation prohibits discrimination against individuals with disabilities in all areas of public life, including jobs, schools, transportation, and all public and private places that are open to the general public.

United Methodists have cause to celebrate. The ADA has been critical for advancing disability justice and works in harmony with the United Methodist pledge to promote "an inclusive, compassionate, and creative response to the needs and gifts of people with disabilities" (Book of Resolutions 3302). In 1990, Church and Society worked in coalition to mobilize support for the passage of the Americans with Disabilities Act.

Our Work Continues

"While there is much to be done within the church to make real the gospel of inclusiveness with regard to people with disabilities, there is a world society that also must be made aware of the concerns and needs of these persons" (Book of Resolutions 3302).

As Rev. Hank Jenkins, Ordained Deacon and Co-Chair of the UM Association of Ministers with Disabilities (UMAMD), shared, "Working toward social justice has always been a strong part of our Wesleyan heritage, and the disabled community must be included in that work. We are proud of our United Methodist leaders and churches who recognize the humanity of people with disabilities and are doing the work to recognize us as full members of the body of Christ."

"Without the ADA, I would have been unable to access the educational and employment resources necessary to live out my calling as a minister of Jesus Christ," said Rev. Jonathan Campbell, Sr. Minister of Lacey UMC in the Greater New Jersey Annual Conference and Co-Chair UMAMD. "Like millions of other Americans, the ADA allowed me to fully use my gifts, live out my dreams, and strengthen my community."

"General Secretaries Table: Statement on Racism," *Faith in Action*, 2020

Editor's Note: This statement was signed by all 13 general secretaries of the general boards and agencies, and calls for dismantling racism. The United States was reckoning with the police killings of George Floyd, Breonna Taylor, and Ahmaud Arbery.

Along with leaders across the church, the General Secretaries of the boards and agencies of The United Methodist Church mark this moment as a time to recommit to urgent action to dismantle racism in the United States and in the church. The recent and callous killings of George Floyd, Breonna Taylor and Ahmaud Arbery while the nation is already reeling from the disproportionate death rates of African American and Native Americans from COVID-19 have rightly sparked anger, lament, protest, and calls for action and reflection. We write to express our own anger, pain and determination to make change in our own spheres of influence and to support the church in the urgent and ongoing work to eliminate racism.

As we are part of a global church, we know that there is racial/ethnic tension and oppression in many nations that must be addressed. Because of the current pain and protests in the United States and its particular history of slavery, Jim Crow and systemic racism, we speak into this context and we appreciate the expressions of solidarity from people around the world.

We know that the disease of racism has infected the United States and the church for much longer than the virus of COVID-19 and that people of color who are women, LGBTQ and differently abled experience overlapping oppressive systems. The Social Principles and the Book of Resolutions are full of statements and calls to action to eliminate institutional racism, acknowledge white privilege and confess the racist practices that permeate our society and the church, to end racial profiling and criminalization of communities of color and to invest ourselves to build new systems based in equity so that all persons may flourish. Neither the agencies, nor the church, has moved with determination from adopting these statements to ordering our work to fulfill them.

We confess that we have work to do in our own agencies. We commit to look with new eyes and renewed commitment at matters relating to staffing, the make-up and leadership of our boards of directors and the allocation of resources to the important work of racial justice and equity. Our current use of tools like tracking racial diversity, applying standards of pay equity and codes of conduct is not enough to transform majority white institutions into places where persons of color are certain that their gifts and talents will be respected and honored. We will do more.

We confess that we have worked individually and in separate programs on the interrelated systems that threaten the lives of African Americans and other people of color. We commit to support each other in the work of elimination of institutional racism and acknowledge that this is the work of the whole church and all of our agencies. While we appreciate the specialized expertise that the General Commission on Religion and Race and others bring to this work, the reformation of the church and the country is not their assignment alone. We commit to bringing our resources to stand beside our constituencies and leaders throughout the church—Annual Conference, district, local church, United Methodist Men, United Methodist Women—to undergird and connect this important work.

We commend the following resolutions, and especially their calls to action, as guidance and input for where and with whom The United Methodist Church can engage anew in this work that we have already said is the church's work to do.

The following excerpts are from the Book of Resolutions, 2016:

Resolution 3376—White Privilege in the United States

We ask each local church with a predominantly white membership:

To reflect on its own willingness to welcome persons without regard to race and to assess the relative accessibility in housing, employment, education and recreation in its community . . .

We challenge individual white persons to confess their participation in the sin of racism and repent for past and current racist practices . . .

Finally, we call all persons, whatever their racial and ethnic heritage, to work together to restore the broken body of Christ.

Resolution 3379—Stop Criminalizing Communities of Color

Call United Methodists to discernment on these issues . . . through the frameworks of human rights, racial justice, and restorative justice.

Engage with churches and local communities in speaking out publicly for police accountability regarding racial profiling, misconduct, abuse and killings.

We pledge to support the church wide focus on *Dismantling Racism: Pressing on to Freedom* that is being developed by leaders across the church.

Chapter Three:

Peace

O ne of the great legacies of the Methodist tradition is its deep commitment to seeking peace. The opening excerpt in this chapter,
from a travel journal called "The Log," recalls the events of the summer
1939 European Youth Seminar. The seminar was made up of a racially
diverse group of young people who traveled across Europe before representing the United States at the World Youth Conference. Days upon
returning from their tour, Britain entered what would be known as World
War II in Europe. The log is a rare look at Methodism's perceptions of the
events of Europe during this time.

Many of the early pieces in this chapter are excerpts from writings
of the Board of World Peace, an exceptional title for a church agency
that reflects the denomination's commitment to peace. Issues of nuclear
disarmament, conscientious objection to war, and concerns for economic
development as a way of peace were issues that were the responsibility
of the Board's work. The Board's peace leaders, including Herman Will
Jr., Rev. Charles F. Boss, Jr., and Rev. Robert McClean, sought to build
relationships across religious and political divisions. In 1955, the Board
remembered the passing of Chief Bull, also known as Richard Sanderville,
who worked on peace issues between the U.S. government and indigenous
communities in Montana. The Board supported diplomatic relationships
with Russia and Eastern Europe in the 1950's at the height of the Cold
War. The Board also spoke out for concern about apartheid in South

Africa as early as the late 1950's. In the beginning of 1962, the Board led a campaign in support of President Kennedy's call to the United Nations for a Race for Peace rather than a race to arms. By the fall of that year, over 30,000 Methodist names on petitions had been delivered to the Kennedy Administration calling for a nuclear test ban treaty and disarmament. As early as 1977, the Board spoke out for strong handgun laws in the U.S., a distant dream currently both in the U.S. and around the world in terms of international arms sales.

After World War II, the call for peace in the midst of war continued to be a priority. From the Cuban missile crisis to the Vietnam war to the war in Iraq to the life-changing events of September 11, 2001, the Board and its predecessor bodies were consistently seeking peace with justice, particularly when engaging the U.S. Administration.

In May 1965, the inter-religious committee on Vietnam met with Secretary of Defense, General Robert McNamara, concerning the war in Vietnam. While interfaith leaders met with the Secretary of Defense, over 500 people of faith gathered at the Pentagon to hold a silent vigil for peace. Both groups expressed a desire for peace in Vietnam and expressed concern for an escalation of war and U.S bombing in North Vietnam.

In the 1980's, the Board of Christian Social Concerns strongly opposed the involvement of U.S. military forces in Central America. The Board advised the denomination when the General Conference voted to speak out for peaceful negotiations during the 1980 Iran hostage crisis. The crisis broke out while General Conference was convening, and the body sent leaders to deliver letters on behalf of the legislative body. The delegation delivered the letter and met with President Carter at the White House and then flew to New York to deliver a message and visit with the Iranian ambassador to the United Nations, Mansour Farhang. Upon a swift delivery, the leaders returned to the session of General Conference to report on its efforts.

In 1986, delegations from both North and South Korea came to the UMB as part of a gathering sponsored by the National Council of Churches on Peace on the Korean Peninsula. The North Korean delegation was the first group of Christians representing their country to visit the United States in more than 50 years.

Of course, one cannot speak about Methodism's commitment to peace without recognizing the immense role Methodism played in the development of the United Nations. Alongside the leadership of Eleanor Roosevelt as the chair of the human rights commission, churches were instrumental in the development of the Universal Declaration of Human Rights—with Methodists in prominent leadership roles:

> The Federal (now National) Council of Churches formed the "Commission on a Just and Durable Peace," chaired by John Foster Dulles, who later became Secretary of State. . . . That group aggressively made approaches to President Roosevelt and other world leaders. . . . Representatives of the churches brought ideas to the governmental bodies at the charter conference in San Francisco and at later UN meetings held in New York.[1]

Excerpts from G. Bromley Oxnam's reflections found below mark the significance of Methodist leadership in the ecumenical movement for peace. The Universal Declaration was approved by the General Assembly in December 1948. Methodists were encouraged to actively study the Universal Declaration in their churches and communities. The World Council of Churches was also formed in 1948 and continues to work for peace today.

Years later, in 1963, the Church Center for the United Nations was completed across the street from the United Nations building. At the dedication ceremony of the building, numerous world leaders and representatives from a variety of faiths (Protestant, Eastern Orthodox, Catholic, and Jewish) gathered to celebrate its completion. UN General Secretary U Thant and US Ambassador Adlai Stevenson, among others, spoke before over 2000 people at the ceremony. The United Women in Faith (formerly titled United Methodist Women) continue to steward the legacy of the building today, and the General Board of Church and Society continues to have an active ministry at the CCUN.

---

1. McClean 1998, 4.

The legacy of peace and reconciliation runs deep in the life of Methodism and continues today. Human rights concerns continue to be a vital part of the agency's witness. Promoting the rights of indigenous peoples and languages across the world, human rights abuses in the Philippines, human rights violations in Israel-Palestine, peace on the Korean Peninsula, and peace efforts on the African continent are of ongoing concern.

"Preface," Charles F. Boss, Jr., *The Log,* 1939

Editor's Note: This entry is from a journal chronicling the experience of youth who traveled around Europe the summer before the U.S. entered World War II.

Although I am writing the Preface I have not read The Log. But I know that when I do read it, I shall find it all written in my heart. For, it will be an inseparable part of you, my companions of days in Europe. The preface, always appearing first in a book is almost always written last. Yet, being last in point of time it serves to introduce—"history." Our Seminar "alpha" stretches back into history and our Seminar "omega," forward into time.

Our Seminar was the first Methodist Youth European Seminar in history. The Amsterdam Conference was the first World Conference of Christian Youth. The Copenhagen Conference was the First conference of European Methodists of the Uniting Conferences of Methodism—visited by a body of American Methodist Youth. The tests of this "history" will measure values still to appear. Even now the European Seminar Youth have spoken in several hundred situations.

High value must be placed upon the enriching experience of our Interracial Fellowship. We are greatly indebted to the Japanese and Negro delegates, without whom our seminar would not have been so rich. Especially are we grateful that the four representatives of the African Methodist Episcopal Zion, and the representative of The Colored Methodist Episcopal Church could be an integral part of the Seminar.

We are indebted to the Board of Education, to the Board of Foreign Missions, and to the National Women's Foreign and Domestic Missionary Societies, and to the members of the National Council of Methodist Youth and The Commission on World Peace for their unstinted co-operation.

Following a thrilling Bon Voyage Dinner the night before, attended by relatives and distinguished guests, the group of 41 on sunny noon of June 28th embarked on the S.S. Aquitania on a new spiritual adventure. (Little did we think that but three months later, the same ship in a new coat of battleship grey would slink out to see past the Statue of Liberty, twelve-pounders mounted on her decks.)

The very first morning at sea the Seminar started in earnest, plunging into the depths of European and American theology, In large groups, in Commissions—sometimes with youth leaders and other times with adult resource leaders, seminar work continued even on the very day we landed back in New York.

Vivid pictures occur to me: of a group of eight or ten in a railway compartment (in Germany) one day, working intently upon serious problems of our youth work; of a small group debating the question of "Danzig" with an officer in the German Labor Camp Service; of earnest conversations with Christians of these other lands as we walked together by the wayside; of earnest youth pressing their questions to European Methodist Bishops, economic experts, authorities on international affairs, leaders of British thought and, anyone willing to help them learn.

The Methodist Youth European Seminar was—shall we say, is—a project in international and interracial friendship and peace. We went to Europe to observe, study, exchange views and widen understanding; to learn more about the Christian Church and especially the Methodist Church in European countries; to come to know the people, become acquainted with youth leaders, and lay the foundations of a world fellowship of Christian youth. Did we succeed? An excellent beginning was made.

There were high spiritual moments, as at Nuremberg. It was during the hour and a half preceding our departure from Berlin. Some fine German youth we had learned to love were with us. As we meditated on the summary of our seminar events up to that time; as part of the Sermon on the

Mount was read from the French New Testament, the twenty-third psalm in German, and as we were lead in prayer in Japanese, our hearts burned within us. In the following silence the Spirit of God came upon us.

"Only in eternity may we renew the bonds of Christian fellowship" which grew during our days in Europe. Yet the glow and tang of these experiences did not dim our minds to the fearful apprehension of war, nor to the serious preparations being made for war:—defense training huts and dug up parks in Paris; solders and tanks and planes in Germany; the blackout of the whole London area—London's life guarded by the "angels" in the sky in the form of "sausage" balloons. We were skirting the edge of an international volcano, almost ready to erupt.

Except for the Church in the United States and its agencies, the European Seminar and attendance at Amsterdam probably would have been impossible. We determined, therefore, to contact Methodist work. What a valuable heritage we bring back from our joint service with Methodists on Sunday in Geneva; our visit to the Methodist hospital in Zurich and the enlightening conference with Bishop Nuelsen; the seminar session with Bishop Melle in Berlin on the state of the Church in Germany and other matters; our contact with Methodist delegates of many lands at Amsterdam, and with the fine group at Copenhagen the Latvian delegates in their colorful native costumes; and last, but not least, those wonderful days at the Wesleyan Shrines and with those genuine British Methodists at North Bank.

But the remembrance of it now brings profound sorrow as we meditate on the fact that some of their nations are now at war. One of our strongest speakers in one London seminar, Canon Stuart Morris (I read but an hour ago) has turned in his clerical orders in the Anglican Church in protest over its attitude on the war.

In København'n we trudged through a drenching rain and came to Christ—a procession of Christians walking in the rain from the Church of the New Jerusalem to the Church of our Lady, where a bishop of the established church conducted the service. Youth sang as we came through the rain with Methodist delegates of twenty European countries—came to kneel before Thorvaldsen's Christ—and ours; came to kneel before a statue of stone where a miracle occurs, occurs when on our knees we have the courage to raise our eyes; then through and through us shines the searching, loving eyes of a Christ who is more than stone. We trudged through the rain in København'n and came to Christ.

This preface is being written during days of intense activity. Days of working to keep the United States out of war. Days of pressing for a neutral bloc of nations to form a continuing mediation conference to bring the war to a close and to lay foundations in conference and negotiation for a just and lasting peace. Days of trying to counsel hundreds—yes, thousands—of interested Methodists who are working for justice and peace.

But, written at the end, the Preface is the beginning, so come with us now to the Port of New York and up the gangplank to the deck of the Aquitania.

If your imagination is still like that of a little child, you will learn of many things perhaps, of «cabbages and kings." We invite you to read the record of these imperishable experiences as they are written in The Log.

"An Exploration of the Problems of a Just and Enduring Peace," G. Bromley Oxnam, When Hostilities Cease: Address and Findings of the Exploratory Conference on the Bases of a Just and Enduring Peace, Commission on World Peace, 1941

Editor's Note: Convener and chairman of the group Bishop Oxnam identifies the key issues to address for global order and peace.

We want no more peace treaties signed in the Hall of Mirrors at Versailles. Humanity desires a permanent peace, not a transient truce. The parade of the bemedaled conquerors has ceased to amuse mankind. Whether it be the strutting Germans of 1870 or the revengeful Allies of 1918, it is seen to be the march of death. It is repentance, not revenge, that is essential to peace. The spirit that characterizes the sincere worshiper must be present when the treaty is signed. It is the worshiper who recognizes that there is one Father of all; that all are members of one family; and that true unity lies in respect for personality and the practice of good will.

The so-called realist, whose irreverent profanity ridiculed an American in the declaration, "Woodrow Wilson talks like Jesus Christ," must be replaced by leaders intelligent enough and practical enough to act like Jesus Christ.

The Communion Table must precede the Conference Table. The bread and the wine of Holy Communion, symbolizing as they do the broken body and shed blood of our Lord, reveal the spirit and the principle upon which permanent peace depends. Men who rise from penitence from the table of the Lord are fit persons to sit in humility at the table of the Peace. Humanity would await the conclusions of such a conference in confidence. But men who march to the treaty table from the blood and hate of battle, who await the coming of their beaten foes in a spirit of revenge, are never peacemakers. They are war-makers who but await the coming of the inevitable evil day.

The fundamental purpose of this Conference is to unite Christian people to the end that the bases of just and enduring peace may be discovered. Its further purpose is to win such support that the social structure of tomorrow may be erected upon these bases. The Methodist Church in this Conference is co-operating with the Federal Council of the Churches of Christ in America. This endeavor, therefore, is one expression of what is believed to be a nation-wide movement upon the part of the Protestant forces of the United States.

It is unfortunate that religious people, who have long enunciated those principles upon which an enduring order may be built, should be divided upon issues of immediate policy rather than united upon issues of ultimate program. That wide differences of opinion exist within the Christian community cannot be denied. There are those whose Christian convictions force them to repudiate war and thus, in conscience, hold to absolute pacifism. There are others who see in the attack of totalitarianism a fundamental threat not only to democracy but to Christianity itself. In conscience, they hold that since there is no international community that can restrain the aggressor and thus exercise force under judicial sanction, they can do no other than to co-operate fully, even to the extent of war, with those who seek to maintain the conditions under which free men may live. It is the belief of those who organized this Conference that it is possible for Christians holding such divergent views to meet as Christians and to respect as well as reject views held by fellow Christians. It is their view that Christians differing as to immediate steps can unite on ultimate goals.

It will be difficult, of course, to rule out all divisive discussions. For instance, are proposals that will assuredly emerge from Christian ethics within the realm of practical politics if Hitler wins? How can Christian bases be laid in a world dominated by Hitler's theory of the state, his racial doctrines, economic plans and projected empire? Can they be applied if English victory should mean the restoration of the Tory and the extension of British imperialism? It is to be hoped that, regardless of these very real difficulties, there may come from this Conference proposals that will incarnate the ideals of our faith, in which we believe lie the possibility of enduring peace.

Is it too much to believe that when the last bomb has been released, and the marauders of the sky cease their piracy; when the last torpedo has found its mark; and the submarine sneaks back to some safe harbor; when the last tank has crashed through gardens once tilled by men of peace; some day, when the light of the morning sun drives night away, man will throw down his weapons and take up his tools? After the bomber comes the builder! What kind of world is man to build?

I.

Such a question calls upon this Conference to explore many areas. Of first importance is that of ideology. What of our faith? Where does value lie? From the beginning, Christianity has affirmed the infinite worth of man. Personality is the supreme good. Men and not things are the goal of social living. In its declaration of the dignity of humanity, Christianity proclaims the fundamental concept upon which democracy is based. In Christian faith, man is of worth because he is a son of God. We are children of one Father. We are brothers. Christianity thus affirms the solidarity of the human family. Ultimate loyalty is not to class, race, or nation.

It is to God. This Conference must re-examine the ideology of Christian faith in the light of contemporary ideologies that repudiate it.

Hermann Rauschning attributes to Adolph Hitler this striking statement relative to the individual: "To the Christian doctrine of the infinite significance of the individual human soul and of personal responsibility, I oppose with icy clarity the saving doctrine of the nothingness and insignificance of the individual human being, and of his continued existence in the visible immortality of the nation. The dogma of vicarious suffering and death through a divine saviour gives place to that of the representative living and acting of the Leader-legislator, which liberates the mass of the faithful from the burden of free will."

Another German, Thomas Mann, declares, "We must define democracy as the form of government and of society which is inspired above every other with the feeling and consciousness of the dignity of man." Mussolini, like Hitler, repudiates this doctrine and likewise the yearning for brotherhood that emerges from it. He says, "Anti-individualistic, the fascist concept is through the state; and it is for the individual so far as he coincides with the state. . . . Liberalism denied the state in the interest of the particular individual . . . for the fascist, everything is in the state, and nothing human or spiritual exists and still less has value outside the state . . . for fascism the state is absolute, before which individuals and groups are relative." Logically, he concludes, "We wish to hear no more about brotherhood . . . because relationships between states are relations of force. . . . Since prehistoric times one shout has come down on the waves of the centuries and the series of generations: 'Woe to the weak.'"

Is that the message of the centuries? Was Jesus mistaken and His sacrifice upon the cross but a sorry gesture? Must we accept the law of the jungle as the law of life, admit that nature is "red in tooth and claw" and, as a part of this cruel order, abandon the practice of love, the hope of liberty, and the dream of abundant life for all?

It is not only a question of the validity of our faith, but a question of the survival of that faith. A new faith is abroad, a faith that cries, "Woe to the weak," a faith that looks upon the individual as but an instrument to be used by the state. The leaders of this faith envision a world ruled by the men of force, supported by loyal technicians. The work of the world is to be done by serflike persons whose fitness to fight has been proved less strong than that of the masters of force.

Certainly the totalitarian doctrine, with its subordination of the individual, is the utter repudiation of the Christian faith, with its exaltation of the person. By what means, if any, can the group become effective enough to withstand the attack of totalitarian force without becoming totalitarian itself?

Frankly, under this question of ideology, the Christian must come to decision on the question, Is this our Father's world?" Is moral purpose written into the nature of things? Was the universe designed for madmen? Does doom await the dictators who strut the stage for a little hour, refusing to repeat the lines of the Eternal Playwright, disregarding the instructions of the Divine Director? Is there to be a final curtain, and are they to hear, "Thou are weighed in the balances, and art found wanting"?

This whole question of ideology must be explored. Is it too much to hope that from the Commission charged with this duty may come an affirmation of our faith that will summon mankind first to its knees and then to its crusade?

"The Significance of December 10," *Methodist Peace Courier*, 1957

Editor's Note: The article commemorates the signing of the U.N. Declaration of Human Rights in 1948, condemns apartheid in South Africa, and invites churches to distribute the U.N. Declaration of Human Rights to their congregations.

"All human beings are born free and equal in dignity and rights. They are endowed with reason and conscience and should act towards one another in a spirit of brotherhood."

(Article 1, UNIVERSAL DECLARATION OF HUMAN RIGHTS)

On December 10, 1948, the General Assembly of the United Nations adopted, without a dissenting vote, the Universal Declaration of Human Rights. Nine years later, the struggle for the rights so nobly and concisely set forth in the Universal Declaration goes on—in India, in the Union of South Africa, in Poland, in Ghana, in the Soviet Union, and in the United States. Few are the nations which have accepted and sincerely practice all of the principles of the Declaration.

We rejoice in the many ways by which the United Nations has advanced human rights during the last twelve years: political freedom to such nations as Indonesia and South Korea, economic and social rights to millions in dozens of underdeveloped countries, assistance to refugees of many nations, defense of Egypt in time of attack, voting rights to women in many Latin American countries, and the release of American prisoners held by the People's Republic of China.

Currently the struggle for the ideals of the Declaration revolves around the tension between human rights and state wrongs! It is between one passage in the Charter which asserts that "nothing contained in the present Charter shall authorize the UN to intervene in matters which are essentially within the domestic jurisdiction of any state" and another passage which affirms that one of the purposes of the organization is to encourage "respect, for human rights and fundamental freedoms."

In this conflict we find the delegates of France walking out of the UN Assembly because of a vote to discuss the status of Algeria, and the Union of South Africa expressing indignation when her treatment of Indians or natives is criticized. The Soviet Union declares that the United Nations should abstain from interference in Hungary, and in the United States the Brickers and Thurmonds cause treaties on human rights to gather dust in committee rooms.

The U. S. Senate should consider on its own merits every treaty on human rights presented to it by the United Nations. The Convention on Genocide, initiated by an American, approved by the Assembly December 9, 1948, and since ratified by 55 nations, should be ratified by us. We know of no good reason why the Convention on the Political Rights of Women should not be approved. It is a shameful retreat from our idealism of the 40's to have our representative on the Commission on Human Rights tell that body that no matter what kind of a Covenant on Human Rights it hammers out, we do not intend to ratify it.

Perhaps the darkest spot on earth for the observance of human rights is the Union of South Africa. Here the Government, the leading political parties, and the laws of the land have increasingly imposed the doctrine of racial superiority on every sphere of human activity. In the past year alone *apartheid*, or racial separation, has been injected by the Government into the churches, the hospitals, and shortly, into the universities.

Therefore, many lovers of freedom in many nations are sponsoring a "Declaration of Conscience" and a Day of Protest, December 10, 1957. This Declaration is an appeal to the conscience of people everywhere to condemn *apartheid* and to demand that the Union of South Africa live up to its obligations under the United Nations Charter.

Concerned persons are invited to add their names to the signers and to help, defray costs of the appeal. Write to Mrs. Franklin D. Roosevelt, Chairman, International Sponsoring Committee . . .

Work for human rights begins in our own hearts and minds, on our streets, and in our churches. In December, Commissions on Christian Social Relations (or World Peace Committees) might appropriately distribute copies of the Universal Declaration of Human Rights at the Official Board meeting, reading several of the articles. The Declaration could be the basis for a discussion in an adult or youth group, and the "Declaration of Conscience" could likewise be used.

"A New Way of Life is Needed," *engage/ social action*, 1973

Editor's Note: Leaders of the church including bishops and agency executives create this statement in response to the end of the Vietnam War, calling on multilateral cooperation through the United Nations, a reduction of military spending, and just and compassionate veteran policies. It also emphasizes the need for government spending to prioritize the basic human needs and ending racism.

We join in expressing our great relief that, at last, the tragic war in Vietnam is drawing to a close, that the bombing and killing and wounding will stop, though the suffering that follows in their wake will be with us for many years. There is no doubt that these deep feelings of relief are shared by hundreds of millions of people around the world.

The deaths of many thousands of human beings, Asians and Americans alike, weigh heavily on our consciences. The devastating effects of the war on the social organization of the Vietnamese people and on the ecology of that relatively small country is a matter of grave concern. This awful toll of death and destruction should also trouble the consciences of all whose decisions dictated the continuation of the struggle. Documented accounts reveal a failure on the part of advisors and officials to raise moral or humanitarian considerations in regard to Vietnam policy. We do not confine the application of these statements to citizens of the United States; however, we do believe that judgment and repentance must begin at home. The United States delegates to the 1972 General Conference of the United Methodist Church felt "moved to confess our continuing complicity in this violence and death," and called the church and the nation to penitence.

Many Americans, including church members, have sought to bind up the wounds of the war victims, to help refugees, the orphans and the maimed, although their accomplishments were often undone by the tactics of war or overshadowed by mushrooming human needs arising from the conflict.

We are glad that the government is now willing to consider new relations with the various political factions in Vietnam and even to contribute to the healing of the wounds of war and to post-war reconstruction in North Vietnam and throughout Indochina. Reconciliation is also urgently needed at home. Everything possible should be done to assist the veterans of the Vietnam war to secure suitable employment and successfully to civilian life. Thoughtful consideration should be given to the return and acceptance of all who resisted the war, both those who left the country and those who entered prison.

We appeal to our leaders to recognize the need for seeking and accepting multilateral judgments and assistance in dealing with international conflict situations. The United Nations should be supported, strengthened, and urged to take greater leadership to the end that the world community may be more effective in averting or halting hostilities in tension areas.

Now is the time for the nation and its leaders to establish new priorities directed to the meeting of human needs. Military spending should be reduced. The nation's resources and energies should be turned to ending poverty and unemployment, to improving health and education, to solving both urban and rural problems, to ending racism and achieving a better future for coming generations. Nothing less than a new way of life is needed at this point in history and we in the churches must bring our contribution to the common task.

Bishop Eugene Slater, San Antonio, TX., president of the United Methodist Council of Bishops; **Bishop Paul A Washburn**, Chicago, Ill., president of the Board of Global Ministries; **Bishop James Armstrong**, Aberdeen, SD., president of the Board of Church and Society; **Bishop James K. Matthews**, Washington, D.C., vice president of Global Ministries for the Division of Ecumenical and Interreligious Concerns; **Bishop John Wesley Lord**, retired, Washington, D.C., executive coordinator of the church's Committee on Peace and Self-Development of Peoples; the **Rev. E. McKinnon White**, Melrose, Mass., vice president of Church and Society for its Division of World Peace, the **Rev. A Dudley Ward**, Washington, D.C., general secretary, Board of Church and Society, **Dr. Herman Will**, Washington, associate general secretary, Division of World Peace.

"Handgun Control," J. Elliott Corbett, *e/sa*, 1975

Editor's Note: This 1975 editorial calls on U.S. Congress to pass legislation to eliminate the private ownership of handguns in response to an alarming rise in handgun ownership and consequent death and violence. Handgun ownership was not made illegal at this time.

Increasingly gun control advocates feel that it is possible over the next few years to eliminate handguns from American society. The latest FBI Crime Report (January through September 1974) shows violent crime has increased 8 per cent.

The handgun is the concealable weapon most often used to commit crimes resulting in death or serious injury. In 1973, 9075 murders were committed through using handguns. Strangely enough, though, 71 per cent of these occurred among people who knew one another—family, friends, neighbors. If handguns were banned from ownership by the American public, it is this latter type of crime—usually resulting from an argument under conditions where a gun is readily available—which would be considerably reduced.

As has been true for the last two Congresses, Senator Hart (D., Mich.) will introduce legislation to ban handguns from sale, ownership, and use in US society except in certain instances. Those exceptions would include the police, the military, and pistol clubs where guns could be kept under secure conditions. In the past legislation has provided reasonable compensation for those who turn in their handguns. However, recently there has been considerable discussion as to whether providing a tax credit might be a more palatable route for an economy-minded Congress. On the House side similar gun legislation has traditionally been offered by Representative Jonathan Bingham (D., N.Y.) and Michael Harrington (D., Mass.).

The 94th Congress has been thought to be a propitious time for passage of handgun control measures for several reasons. This Congress will be more liberal than its predecessors. Violent crime continues to go on. The recession will not soften the trend. . . .

There are a lot of guns in the hands of the public in the United States. The Eisenhower Commission in 1968 estimated that there were at least 40 million handguns in America. There are more now. That Commission presented an interesting report on handgun sales. They noted that between 1899 and 1948 there were two and one-half million guns sold per decade. From 1949 to 1958, this number of such sales almost doubled reaching 4.8 million. During the next decade, 1958 to 1968, handgun sales doubled again, totaling 10.2 million, and from 1962 to 1968 the sales of handguns quadrupled.

We are a nation armed to the teeth. The Eisenhower Commission in 1968 estimated that there are about 210 million guns owned by American citizens—or roughly one gun for each person.

In the kind of crime-ridden society Americans find themselves in, isn't it necessary to keep a gun in the house for protection? This reasoning disavows the fact that 99 per cent of home burglaries occur when no one is at home. So the householders "protection" does him no good. In fact, the likelihood is that the gun itself will be stolen along with other household goods! 500,000 guns are stolen each year in America.

But more important, a gun in the home, if used, is more likely a [sic] kill a member of the family than a burglar. A study of firearms use in Cuyahoga County, Ohio, an area including Cleveland and its suburban area, was conducted in 1973 by members of the Case Western Reserve University Medical School. The results show that from 1958 to 1972 only seventeen burglars, robbers, or intruders were killed by guns in the hands of persons who were protecting their homes. In the same period six times as many firearm fatalities occurred in the home while at least 1000 to 2000 serious non-fatal firearm accidents also occurred during those four years.

. . .

Some may say that making guns illegal will not stop the criminals from getting them. That is partly true. Most of the guns used by professional criminals were stolen from other owners. If the supply were dried up, guns could less easily be stolen or purchased on the street.

Another factor not often recognized is that those involved in crime often commit petty offenses. They may, for instance, be stopped for a traffic violation. The police could search the glove compartment or the trunk and come upon a store of handguns. These would be lifted and the general supply of firearms decreased. After a while it would be pretty hard to get a gun.

The time has come to eliminate private ownership of handguns.

"Conference Acts on Iran Crisis: A Call for Reconciliation," *e/sa*, 1980

Editor's Note: This set of letters and report are an account of the 1980 General Conference's efforts to call for peace between the U.S. and Iran in the midst of the General Conference meeting At the time, fifty-twp American diplomats and citizens were held hostage by Iranian students who supported the Iranian Revolution. The account demonstrates the role Church and Society played in facilitating and supporting the UMC's diplomacy effort during the crisis.

In a setting dominated by proposed changes in the *Book of Discipline* and general church programs for the next four years, the 1980 General Conference was unable to put aside matters of the real world as Iran-related events persistently commanded the attention of the delegates.

The series of events began on April 17 with an optional issue briefing on Iran sponsored by the Board of Church and Society. At that briefing, two United Methodist clergymen who had held Easter services with hostages reflected on their experiences. Also, Professor Norman Forer of the University of Kansas asserted that a military action by the United States simply would unite the squabbling Iranian students and government and drive Iran into the Soviet camp. Bishop Dale White of the New Jersey area, who had visited Iran in December, said that the filthy Americans confined in the Embassy are not the only hostages, but also the thousands who were brutalized and terrorized under the Shah.

The next day, Bishop White reported to the body of the Conference on that Christmas day visit and called on United Methodists to be the "first major Christian body to send a conciliatory message to the Ayatollah Khomeini" and to send a delegation to the White House to "counsel the utmost patience and restraint."

1980, Delegation to White House

- Bishop Roy C. Nichols—President, Council of Bishops; episcopal leader. Pittsburgh, Pa. Area.

- Bishop C. Dale White—episcopal leader, New Jersey Area; member, Board of Discipleship; one of a group of clergy who visited Iran in late December and spoke with the Ayatollah Khomeini on Christmas Day.

- Mai (Mrs. C. Jarrett) Gray—Kansas City, Mo. President, Women's Division, and vice-president, Board of Global Ministries. Member of Missouri West delegation.

- James M. Dolliver—Olympia, Wash. A Washington State Supreme Court Justice. Member of Pacific northwest delegation, and chairperson of Legislative Committee on Church and Society.

- Jack Bremer—staff member of the ecumenical campus ministry at the University of Kansas, Lawrence, Kan. Was one of three clergy who conducted worship services for the American hostages in Tehran on Easter.

- Christopher Mitchell—Shelby, N.C. A member of the Western North Carolina delegation. One of the presenters of the Laity Address on April 16. Former chairperson of the National Youth Ministry Organization. A sophomore at Duke University.

- Bishop William R. Cannon—episcopal leader of the Georgia Area. Member of Board of Publication. A president of the World Methodist Council. Offered the prayer at Mr. Carter's inauguration as President.

- D. W. Brooks—Atlanta, Ga. Member of the North Georgia delegation. Considered founding father of the Ministerial Education Fund concept that has resulted in millions of dollars in support of ministerial education. Friend and advisor to President Carter.

Message to President Carter from the General Conference of the United Methodist Church

April 23, 1980

We the delegation from the General Conference of the United Methodist Church, 1,000 delegates representing more than 10 million people in the United States and around the world, bring greetings to you, our President, from that body, and say, "Grace and peace be with you from our Lord and Savior Jesus Christ."

We regret that you were unable to address the General Conference, but we are grateful that you are willing to receive us on what we believe to be a most serious and urgent mission.

We commend you and your administration for the restraint you have shown in the present crisis with Iran. We admire your patience and the tireless efforts you have exerted to reach an agreement with the Iranian government, in order both to free the American hostages and to normalize relations with Iran.

The General Conference has asked us to come to you, "to counsel the utmost patience and restraint." We do urge you, despite the frustration, even exasperation, of attempting to negotiate with a government still in process of formation, to continue the same constructive and peaceful endeavor you have pursued thus far, for we sincerely believe that in due season you will reap the fruits of your well-doing, if you faint not.

While the American people are angry and distressed by the current impasse, we believe that at heart we are a reasonable and a generous people. A vast reservoir of support exists in our land, especially among the churches and synagogues, for policies which make for peace. The women and men of our denomination have long been concerned for questions of international justice and human rights.

We implore you, Mr. President, in the name of the Prince of Peace, not to give in to those who counsel military intervention, nor to take steps which will lead eventually to war. To do so will create a state of affairs far worse than the one we now face. Not only would the lives of the hostages be forfeited, but the lives of countless thousands of Iranian and American people would be sacrificed, and the peace and stability of the world put in grave jeopardy.

We urge a course of action which will restore normal diplomatic relationships with Iran as soon as possible, and which will lead to reconciliation and a new friendship based upon respect and mutuality of interest. The General Conference implores you "to offer assurances to Iran that we will honor their national independence and assist them in their struggle for a balanced, just, and sustainable economy." We cannot identify with policies of covert or overt intervention in the affairs of that nation. The

Iranian people have demonstrated that they will not support a government which is not of their own choosing or representative of their long-range interests. Surely we should be the first to honor such a spirit.

We fervently believe, Mr. President, that reconciliation with the Iranian people is still possible. We share a common faith in God and respect for moral values. Tens of thousands of Iranians have studied in this country and have returned to assure their families of our good sense and our good will. Strong and capable leaders are struggling there amid the chaos and suffering of a nation being born, to bring unity to a diverse people and tranquility to an aroused people. We have in common vital commercial and geopolitical interests. Surely this strong foundation upon which an edifice of friendship may be built ought not to be eroded by actions taken hastily and in the heat of passion.

We assure you of our confidence, Mr. President, as you take steps to diffuse this crisis, to allow the grievances of both sides to be aired and the interests of both nations acknowledged and assured of fruition. We pledge to do everything in our power to mobilize the faith community behind a policy of restraint. Our prayers and the prayers of our people are with you.

May God grant you wisdom and strength.

Message to the General Conference from President Carter

I appreciate the concern demonstrated by the General Conference of the United Methodist Church in sending a delegation to meet with me and to deliver a message concerning the holding of 50 of your fellow citizens in Iran by a group of terrorists. The United States has explored every avenue to find a peaceful solution to this crisis. Unfortunately, for more than five months, the leaders of Iran have been unwilling to fulfill their responsibilities and obligations as a government to put an end to a situation which has been condemned by virtually every nation in the world.

I also deeply appreciate your offer of prayers and support as we face the difficult decisions of the days ahead. We have offered the hand of peace and friendship to the people of Iran, but the kind of relationship of mutual respect which we seek cannot develop while innocent Americans are being held prisoner.

Message to President Carter

April 25, 1980

We the delegates of this quadrennial General Conference of the United Methodist Church representing the church in 23 nations, reaffirm our message of April 23, 1980, delivered by a delegation of eight United Methodist leaders to the President of the United States. In the light of the events of the past twenty-four hours we again insist that reconciliation and restraint are indivisible and that the peoples of the world long for peace with justice. We urge the leaders of the United States and Iran to stand against the counsel of those who advise any form of violence.

Again, we request President Carter and Congress to offer the Iranian people assurances that we honor their national independence and will assist them in "their struggles for a balanced, just and sustainable economy," and at the same time we request the Iranian leaders and people to release the United States' hostages.

Our hearts and prayers go out to the families of those who died or were injured "in a remote desert area of Iran" even as we continue prayerfully to support the hostages and their families. The restraint which appears to be shown on all sides in reaction to the most recent event in this continuing tragedy gives us hope that we may indeed stand on the threshold of new opportunities for peaceful solutions to this wrenching crisis. We plead for openness on the part of both nations, acknowledgment of fault on the part of both nations, and the resumption of conciliatory dialogue between the leaders of both nations. In the sorrow of the moment we celebrate the gifts of grace and hope and pray for new beginnings.

Message to the Ayatollah Imam, Khomeini, President Abolhassan Bani-Sadr, and the people of Iran

In the name of God the merciful, the compassionate. In the name of Jesus Christ, our loving and forgiving Lord. Amen.

We, the General Conference of the United Methodist Church, religious leaders who care about the poor and oppressed in the United States and the world, meeting in Indianapolis, Indiana, U.S.A., hear the agonies of your people; we hear their cries for freedom from foreign domination, from cultural imperialism, from economic exploitation.

We long for that time when our peoples may dwell together in peace.

In the words of Moses, the liberator, let us say to each other, "Let my people go!" And let us begin to walk together down the long, hard road toward reconciliation.

"We Say NO to Contra Aid!"
Mary Council-Austin, *e/sa*, 1986

Statement by the Rev. Mary Council-Austin delivered on the steps of the U.S. Capitol to participants in the People's Filibuster against the War in Nicaragua.

My brothers and sisters, I join you today with a profound grief and sense of outrage that the House of Representatives approve President Reagan's request to escalate the unjust war against Nicaragua. I join you in saying no!—to any aid, but especially military aid to the contra forces. I join you in saying no!—to what has become an open declaration of war on Nicaragua, a tiny nation of three million people, half of whom are under 16 years of age.

Martin Luther reminds us that war, my friends, is the greatest plague that can affect humanity; it destroys religion; it destroys states; it destroys families. Any scourge is preferable to it. As one who stands in the Christian tradition, I am persuaded that the God of peace is never glorified by human violence. We say no today because nothing can be politically right that is morally wrong; we say no—because no necessity can ever sanctify a law that is contrary to equity.

We say no!—out of our heritage of freedom and democracy. We say no!—to our government taking that option of violence and death. We say no!—to the double talk about or concern for justice and human rights while we base our foreign policy on war. As a Christian, I am here today with you, my brothers and sisters, to send a word of hope to the people of Nicaragua—as we say yes to the right to choose; to say yes to the good news of your involvement in building a new society of the people and for the people . . . to say yes, as we sense a desire to involve your religion community in giving shape to your identity.

I call upon you, my sisters and brothers, to lift your voices now!—and we say no!—until our government repents, until we are lifted to the higher course of justice in a world in which swords will be turned into plowshares, nations will seek war no more, and in which people in every nation will be regarded with dignity.

"Torn by the Contradictions of War in the Middle East," Thom White Wolf Fassett, *Christian Social Action*, 1991

General Secretary issues statement in response to the Persian Gulf war.

Today, as people of faith, we are moved to tears, torn by the contradictions of war in the Middle East and mourning our collective inability to live together on this planet.

We mourn the brutality of violence.

We mourn the loss of all precious human life.

We mourn the price the earth itself must pay as it struggles to keep us all alive.

We mourn questionable polices of all nations which would seek superiority over others.

All people of faith must come together in prayer petitioning for the softening of the hearts of those who would seek mutual destruction, begging for the release of our captivity in violence and seeking the incarnation of love which is our eternal hope.

It is imperative that we petition world leaders to bring a cessation to hostilities, to end the conflict speedily without deploying massively destructive weapons and to assure the world that the "Geneva Conventions" will be strictly observed for the relief and protection of refugees.

We must activate our prayer chains and continue our prayer vigils so as to create, in our own lives, the witness of the power of God in the world and our continued ability to live the witness of love.

In the aftermath of the hostilities in the Middle East, we express corporate and pastoral concern for both civilian and military populations of all countries engaged in or subject to the violence of war.

At the same time, we decry another kind of violence now being reported on an hourly basis regarding the suspension of civil liberties for persons who are reported to be Arab-Americans. Because of the fear of terrorism, Arab-Americans are reported to be under suspicion and are subject to practices by agents of the federal government which have reportedly deprived them of their civil rights.

While mindful of the clear need to be vigilant regarding the security of all and understanding the potential for terrorism, we decry any acts of racism which discriminate against a national grouping of peoples in the United States during these most critical times.

We call local congregations to reach out to our Arab-American neighbors for peace and understanding. We call upon all persons of faith to unite hands and hearts to begin the healing of a nation and the world.

"To Follow the Way of Peace," Dallas Darling, *Christian Social Action*, 1991

Editor's Note: Church and Society was the successor of a long tradition of supporting conscientious objectors. The following account is from a veteran of the 1990-1991 Gulf War, in which the U.S. led against Iraq.

From the article: A member of the inactive reserves activated for Desert Storm reflects on why he has become a conscientious objector.

I grew up in Kansas and was raised in an environment where there was quite a lot of racism, war mentality and blind patriotism. It was the type of environment where people never questioned the government.

I came from a poor family, and, when I got out of high school, one of the ways to pay for my education was to go through the ROTC program in Pittsburgh, Kansas. I was told all the great things about the army—how it helped recruits "be all you can be" and how it paid for their education. I never realized there was another side.

Then some things woke me up. When the Iranian air bus was shot down, I remember everybody was cheering about that action. I thought of my commitment to Christ, and I realized I wasn't really following the teachings of Christ.

While in college, I attended a debate that dealt with war and peace. The debate was between a Church of the Brethren pastor, who expounded the peaceful stance of Christ, and an Assembly of God pastor, who presented the just war stance. For the first time I really thought more about the Sermon on the Mount and how Christ taught that we should love our enemies and what it means to be a peacemaker as a child of God.

Would You Ever Kill?

I asked my instructor, who had served in the Vietnam War, "Sir, would you, as a Christian, ever kill, or do you think it is possible for Christians to go to war?" This 40-year-old man began to weep as he told me that in Vietnam he took part in eradication of villages. He was a captain on a gun ship, and he remembered shooting women and children. As he shared that experience with me, I could see the pain it caused.

After college, I began to work in several homeless missions, and I really began to understand the God of life who promotes justice, peace, and wholeness for everybody. Later I served as a youth pastor and an associate pastor of an Assembly of God church in Kansas, and that's when my theology began to change. I started to speak out because a nearby trailer court had a lot of poor children and we would bus them in every Sunday to tell them about Jesus, but we would never do anything about their social or economic conditions. So I began to speak about how we need to be more involved socially, and I was forced to take a vow of silence. I knew then that it was time to change denominations, and I appreciated the United Methodist broad-mindedness and the ability to be able to share and discuss some of these concerns.

As a pastor in rural Kansas, I am faced every year with seeing families move from their farms—seeing a breakdown in families and the hurt and hopelessness that causes. In rural America whole communities of 1,500 or less are dying out. I began to see the contradictions in the situation— farmers growing all the food but receiving inadequate economic revitalization to avoid being wiped out. So I really began to question.

I had lived a very individualistic and privatized religion. I prayed, went to church, and went out to save peoples' souls. Then I began to realize that the way I live affects my brothers and sisters all around the world. I think that's what real biblical faith is—that, as a church, as a community, as a people of God, we are committed to living a dangerous Christianity that helps people everywhere.

During this time I was in the inactive reserves. I had served in the infantry for a while, but my beliefs about killing another individual were incompatible with infantry objectives, so I thought one way to get out was to become a chaplain in the army. However, I was turned down because they thought some of my views were too political, especially my view about so many billions of dollars going into weapons.

Early last year I went down to Guatemala. There I worked among the people, listened to them, and heard about some of the US activity down there including training some of the right wing death squads. After that I talked with friends in the military who had served on special forces and who had trained some of those squads to protect our "national self-interest."

I Could No Longer Serve

When I got back from Guatemala, I indicated that I could no longer serve in the military. I always thought, when I signed my papers to become an officer in the army, that, if I ever wanted to get out, or if something else happened, I could pay back the ROTC money. I even offered to pay it back, and they said they would send me the paper work.

In August I had an opportunity to go to Washington, D.C. There I heard about some of the reasons we wanted a war: to establish a military base in the Middle East since we lost our base when the Shah of Iran was toppled; to try out our high-tech weapons to see how effective they were; to kick the Vietnam syndrome; to keep the Pentagon defense budget from being slashed; to control the oil for economic reasons. I knew I didn't want to participate in such a war, so I took part in some anti-war demonstrations.

When I made a statement that appeared in the paper saying that I was more frightened of George Bush than Saddam Hussein, I received a death threat a couple of days later. I began to realize that when a person speaks out in this nation, it can be dangerous. In fact, it is risky to follow the way of peace as Christ taught.

Then last fall I received notification that I was being activated for Desert Storm and had to go to Fort Ben Harrison in Indiana. There we trained troops. The first few weeks we were there, they said some of us would be going to the Gulf, but the war was over real soon, so I served out my time in Indiana. I never went to Saudi Arabia; that would have been a real hard decision. I don't think I would have gone, and that would have meant a court martial.

Church Not Prepared

I attempted to get help from my denomination, but I think that some of the leadership was afraid to speak out, or some may have been fairly sympathetic toward the war action. When I went to Fort Ben Harrison, I met another United Methodist minister, a college campus minister, who also felt that the United Methodist Church was not prepared to deal with the issue of conscientious objectors.

It was a struggle for me to leave my wife and the three churches that I serve—against my will and my beliefs. It was a real frustrating time. Most of the people in the three churches were very supportive. As a matter of fact, one lady said, "Dallas, I'll be out there protesting; just tell me what you want me to do." That was solidarity. That was someone willing to put her life on the line. So many times we can submit papers, we can preach, we can talk, we can have conventions, but until we act, all that is really worthless. There comes a time when the church needs to act.

While I was at Fort Ben Harrison, I did file for CO status, but they held my package until my tour of duty was ended. One of the things that is dehumanizing when you file for CO status, is that you have to go to the mental health clinic where they analyze you. An individual attempting to live a peaceful life, one who doesn't want to kill anybody, is analyzed whereas people who make nuclear weapons, for instance, are not.

On a recent Sunday, I told my congregation that patriotism is not going and fighting and giving your life for your country, whether the cause is just or unjust. Patriotism is doing what God wants us to do—working for peace and helping our families and everybody else have education, homes, enough food, and so forth. The biggest danger I see facing the North American church today is not the new age movement or homosexuality; instead it is confusing the kingdom of God with the American way of life and US nationalism. God's kingdom and nationalism are diametrically opposed and very contradictory.

We seem to major on the minors and minor on the majors. We will fight and bicker over the color of the church carpet or walls or on whether to start a pre-school program, yet all around us thousands are dying of starvation, war and economic exploitation. I think sometimes that God is awfully embarrassed by the church. It is time that we follow the Christ of life, the Christ found in one another.

The United Methodist Church today needs to be consistent. If it's going to be against any kind of death, it needs to promote life, whether it deals with the environment, with people, or with starvation in our country or overseas. We need to have a consistent life ethic. For instance, if individuals are concerned about abortions in America, they need to be just as concerned about the 40,000 babies who die every year before reaching their first birthday, and about the amount of money going to the Pentagon, which causes tremendous death and destruction to Third World countries.

I believe that if we talk war and live to go to war, there will be war. However, if we talk peace and live peace, then there will be peace.

"Publisher's Column: September 11th, 2001," Jim Winkler, *Christian Social Action*, 2001

Editor's Note: On September 11, 2001, Islamic extremists hijaked four commercial airplanes. Two planes struck New York City's Twin Towers, one struck the Pentagon in Arlington, Virginia, and a fourth landed in a field in Shanksville, Pennsylvania. Nearly 3,000 people were killed, and responses to acts of terrorism became a dominant priority of the US government. The General Secretary Jim Winkler recounts the experience of staff on that day.

Staff of the General Board of Church and Society gathered for prayer on the morning of September 11. We were all stunned and upset. Following prayer, most staff was sent home. Police officers passing by the United Methodist Building told us that an airliner was heading for the U.S. Capitol, directly across the street. Lawmakers, lobbyists and visitors were moving away from the Capitol as quickly as they could. Rumors were rife that the Capitol and the State Department had been bombed.

As people left the building we hugged one another and exchanged meaningful looks. We locked the front doors. All federal buildings on the Hill were evacuated. Soon, Capitol Hill was silent except for sirens. Police officers lined 1st Street, NE. We moved a water cooler to the lobby and invited officers in to use our facilities and call their loved ones. The United Methodist Building offered a ministry of hospitality.

In the days that followed, we held special prayer services in Simpson Memorial Chapel. We mourned and grieved for those who died and we gave thanks to God that the Capitol was spared. It is impossible to know what damage the United Methodist Building might have incurred had the Capitol been hit.

Prior to the tragic events of September 11, 2001, the date had already been important to me because of another tragedy. On that date in 1973, the democratically elected government of Chile, headed by President Salvador Allende, was overthrown by General Augusto Pinochet with the full knowledge, connivance, and covert support of the United States government and our secret police, officially known as the Central Intelligence

Agency. The horrendous and disastrous ramifications of that illegal coup continue to haunt the people of Chile and will forever remain a stain on the United States of America.

Each September 11th I made it a point to observe the day by speaking with a Chilean friend of mine whose father was forced into exile by the dictator Pinochet. Later her father served honorably as Chile's Ambassador to the United States when democracy was restored. I will continue to remember Chile on September 11 in the future as I also will honor the victims of the terror attacks on the United States. I encourage everyone to hold these two tragic events in their hearts on future anniversaries.

I believe completely that God is with us in this time. I believe God's love will prevail. As Uri Avnery said shortly after the attacks, "Instead of the destroyed New York edifices, the twin towers of Peace and Justice must be built."

"Congolese Bishop visits GBCS," Mark Harrison, *Faith in Action*, 2006

Editor's Note: Church and Society's Mark Harrison related with faith leaders on the African continent to monitor and support US aid for international development in the region. This article relates the ongoing relationship between United Methodist leaders of the Democratic Republic of Congo and Church and Society.

Bishop David K. Yemba from the Democratic Republic of the Congo visited the General Board of Church and Society on June 13-14.

He serves as national president of the Civil Society of Churches and Religious Communities.

Yemba gave us an update on present situation in the Congo. We discussed ways GBCS can work with the Central Congo Conference.

The conflict in DRC has killed 4 million people since 1998. A transition government is now in place with the first free elections in 40 years scheduled for July 30. GBCS gave a Peace with Justice grant of $5,000 to the West Congo Annual Conference to help train 100 election observers in each annual conference and inform people about democratic values for the upcoming national election process. The people of the DRC need peace, democracy and equitable economic development. Please keep them in your prayers.

Yemba met with Mark Lippert, foreign policy advisor to Sen. Barack Obama, (D-Ill). Obama introduced the Democratic Republic of the Congo Relief, Security and Democracy Promotion Act (S. 2125). The legislation requires the U.S. government to promote the political process in the Congo by the appointment of a special envoy, and to provide economic assistance and humanitarian relief. The Senate Foreign Relations Committee has approved the bill. Yemba expressed his support for the legislation and appreciation to Obama for his concern for the people of the Congo.

A GBCS delegation visited the Democratic Republic in 2003.

"Death, Disappearance and Despair: A Korean American's Reflection on 'Called Seminar: El Salvador,'" Miok Fowler, *Faith in Action*, 2019

Editor's Note: As part of the educational program, Church and Society developed an immersion trip to El Salvador, looking at the push-pull factors of migration. One of the participants offered a reflection on the journey.

Miok Fowler, Ed. D., participated in the 2019 Called Seminar to El Salvador.

El Salvador is a country not unlike my homeland of Korea. Both were brutalized by dictatorship, endured civil war, shared bitter ties to the Cold War, and sustained post-war periods fraught with corruption and physical and intellectual oppression.

I was just 4-years old in 1950 when the Communist-backed Northerners of Korea invaded their brother's land to the South where our home was. I was 7 by the time when the fighting had ended and nearly 3 million people had been slaughtered. The Korean war had never technically ended, and in my youth I thought it never would. The inhumane living conditions, the food shortages, the disappearance of neighbors and friends, the rape and violence—those are the experiences that form the fleshy grooves and patterns on the finger pads of survivors.

In the summer before the fall General Board of Church Society's "More to Migration" seminar in El Salvador, Oscar Albert Martinez Ramirez placed his 23-month-old daughter, Angie Valeria, on his back, underneath the black t-shirt he wore, her little arms around his neck, as he tried to swim from Mexico to Texas. Ramirez, his wife and daughter were leaving behind the gang ravaged home of El Salvador. They were looking away from graft scandals and economic strife towards a life that promised fruitful labor and dignity in the United States.

Current U.S. policy is suspicious of those migrating from the south to our borders. But their stories, and mine, are, at the core, the most American of stories as they come. I'm reminded of Rose of Sharon, the eldest daughter of the Joads in Steinbeck's Grapes of Wrath. Following the 1930s economic despair brought by the Dust Bowl, the Joads set out for a life of dignity in California. But the journey, riddled with hunger and malnutrition resulted in the stillborn birth of Rose of Sharon's child. Oscar Ramirez and his daughter would meet a similar fate as their lifeless bodies would be found later washed up on the shores of the Rio Grande.

But the spirit of the Salvadoran people is not broken. At the NGO sites we visited, with little resources, commerce, healthcare and education are advanced like weapons sharpened for war. Stories of Archbishop Oscar Romero are plentiful as solidarity is nurtured with his words against social injustice, poverty, political extremism, torture and militia government rule. El Salvador's Archbishop Romero's life, like many civil rights leaders, was cut short by an assassination.

John Steinbeck wrote to Martin Luther King Jr. on September 28, 1958 after a set back in MLK's struggle. Steinbeck described the set back as a time for evaluation and reevaluation and wrote,

"… I am sorry for your pain but very sure that you accept it as a part of the pattern without which no human step toward dignity and understanding is ever taken."

So true does that ring for the Archbishop Romero.

The story of El Salvador is a human story. It is a war story. It is my story. It is an American story. As Dorothy Kazel, the murdered nun by the El Salvadorian militia government once wrote: "Waiting, hoping and yearning for peace." Yes, indeed, the peace, freedom and democracy will find the place for Salvadorans.

Chapter Four:

Economy and Ecology

The 1908 MEC's Social Creed reflects a deep commitment to economic justice within the Wesleyan tradition. The creed called for, among other issues, a living wage, the abolishment of child labor, the establishment of safety standards, and the right to arbitration among industrial dissensions. Decades later, the Church continued to raise alarms concerning the economic life of God's people. In 1976, the General Conference declared world hunger a "missional priority," instructing agencies across the denomination to address the issue. In response, Church and Society developed resources and networks to advocate for just and equitable production and distribution of food. Its task was to address the root causes of hunger and advocate for policies founded on the principles that food is a human right.

Organizing efforts for workers is a strong and clear commitment in twentieth century Methodism. Quite famously, Cesar Chavez delivered a telegram to the 1972 General Conference expressing his appreciation for United Methodist support of the United Farm Worker (UFW) organizing movement. The organization and its predecessor bodies supported farmworkers wanting to improve labor conditions in the work of picking grapes, tomatoes, and other products. A 1986 theological statement from the Economic Boycott Task Force of The United Methodist Church issued a call to the Church to take a stand. In it, the Church outlines how boycott is a means of nonviolent resistance against exploitation, and that the Church is called to be a healing, prophetic voice for those most marginalized and impacted by poverty and hunger.

Beginning in 1999, The United Methodist Church supported a boycott of Mt. Olive Pickle Company by the Farm Labor Organizing Committee. The General Board of Church and Society worked with the NCC, the North Carolina Annual Conference and others to support the boycott. Finally, in 2004, Mt. Olive Pickle Company and FLOC signed two agreements. One was to allow guest workers—who are largely Hispanic immigrants—the right to collective bargaining. The second included promising increased prices to cucumber growers, provide increased support for providing workers' compensation insurance coverage, and expand its code of conduct for North Carolina's suppliers and growers.

The commitment to labor rights extends as well to the Board's practices. In 1983, the agency's Board of Directors meeting in Memphis, Tennessee, moved hotel conference centers in response to a picket line that had formed outside the hotel that the agency had planned to use.

Economic justice was seen early on as the key to peace. Military advancement requires a lot of resources that could otherwise provide hospitable and livable conditions for all of humankind, including adequate food supply, housing, and educational opportunities. The understanding of the relationship between international development and peace efforts even led in 1971 to two former staff members, J. Elliott Corbett and Luther E. Tyson, to develop an investment firm, Pax World Fund, the first broadly diversified, publicly available mutual fund to use ethical as well as financial screens in its investment decisions.

The Church has long seen how the federal budget is a moral document. Government funding reflects the values of society particularly in how we support our communities in addressing hunger, poverty, and housing for the flourishing of all our neighbors. Today, the federal budget—particularly allocations for military spending—continues to be a critical issue.

The struggle to reconcile the demand for natural resources and the care for God's creation is ever more urgent. Public policies to address environmental racism, the climate change crisis, and natural resources is a central concern. As early as the 1950's, Methodist social action saw extraction industries as detrimental both to future generations and to marginalized communities. The inter-related nature of environmental, economic justice and peace further became an issue that the denomination's Council of Bishops addressed in their historic 1986 pastoral and foundations document In Defense of Creation: The Nuclear Crisis & a Just Peace and then later in the 2009 document God's Renewed Creation: Call to Hope & Action. The latter document's development was supported and developed with the Methodist Building as the location for the project's coordination.

The 1986 document was re-published in June 1986 by the Board. It lifted up critical points that the Bishops raised about the intersection of poverty, nuclear arms, and the environment:

> Justice is abused in the overwhelming power of nuclear-weapon states to threaten the self-determination, the security, and the very life of nonaligned and non-belligerent nations because nuclear hostilities are bound to have devastating environmental and human consequences for the whole earth.[1]

In more recent years, Church and Society has actively witnessed to the realities of climate change. Staff and partners have called on the federal and global levels of decision makers to address the crisis, insisting that any decisions include communities that are most impacted globally, including the Philippines, the U.S.-Mexico border, and regions of Africa.

While the call for economic justice and care for the environment continues, it is important to consider in this chapter the agents of change that are highlighted, in particular the authors of the later articles. These changemakers include women and young people whose voices have become more prominent.

"Getting Stewardship Out of Knee-Pants," *Methodist Peace Courier*, 1958

Editor's Note: This article reflects on the United States' energy use, military costs, consumption, and production and how they all relate to the stewardship of natural resources.

---

1. Council of Bishops 1986, 12.

Stewardship—a peace concern? Hardly, if the conventional notion persists that it is how one uses his money and how much he gives his church.

At least two further aspects of stewardship have been raised; what we owe to others, which usually ends in a summons to share, and in agricultural regions, soil and conservation.

In an industrial society the issues are less clear, although noble beginnings have been made concerning fair labor practices, adequate working and living conditions, and certain other domestic problems treated in our Social Creed.

But the full extension of stewardship challenges peace advocates today. What about the effects of our military effort on our prosperity? What about the "economics of peace making?" Consider the utilization of raw materials and basic resources necessary to maintain our desired standard of living.

The serious extension of stewardship to include the well-being of all mankind has not sufficiently occupied the mind and thought of the Church. If you care, you will share; we are told. But what if sharing is already too late as a starting point in the whole process? What precedes benevolence?

. . .

Can we Americans ever really sense the elemental human problem again? In a world where:

1. More people live in huts of mud and straw than in any other kind of shelter.

2. More travel on their own two feet than on all mechanized means of transport.

3. More people have a life expectancy under 30 years than over.

4. More mothers watch their children die in infancy than see all their offspring reach mature years.

5. More people live without medical aid than know the attention of nurse or doctor.

6. More people do not know what it means to vote than have ever cast even a single ballot.

Our scientific and technical advances have dulled our minds to the fact that more people are hungry, ill-clad and poorly housed than there were in 1900. And tomorrow the story will be worse despite the progress in many newly-developed countries. These realistic truths demand interpretation in terms of Christian stewardship.

Stewardship, furthermore, is the extension of Christian concern into the future. What of those who come after us?

A cardinal problem, of course, is the possible genetic damage from radioactivity, particularly from bomb tests. But that has been treated so adequately elsewhere that we turn our attention to a different problem.

Less spectacular, but perhaps no less important, is the use of basic resources to expand our advanced standard of living, and especially for the gigantic military preparations of the USA and USSR. To canvass this problem is a stewardship challenge to proponents of peace. Let us take but one aspect of it.

To maintain our way of life and its pleasures the American people consume the basic potential of several oncoming generations. Add to this the military effort, and it can be conservatively stated that we are utilizing ten or a dozen times the basic mineral and fuel deposits to which one generation is entitled.

New energy from atomic and heavy hydrogen processes, providentially discovered near the end of the fossil fuels, provides us with limitless sources of power. But power must be applied to substance in an industrial society.

Easily accessible and high-grade ores are slowly disappearing. Six times as much ore must be processed today to obtain a given amount of copper as in 1900. A similar condition holds with reference to taconites for iron and bauxite for aluminum. There is no cause for alarm as to a scarcity of such elements; their presence in common basalt is limitless. But the cost of processing them is quite another matter.

Ordinary igneous rock contains per hundred tons, 8 tons of aluminum, 5 tons of iron, 180 pounds of manganese, 40 pounds of nickel, 20 pounds of copper and 4 pounds of lead. In the foreseeable future our grandchildren will be reducing the old granite of our vast mountain ranges for their industrial needs at a tremendous cost in energy and equipment.

Meanwhile, as Christians, to how much of the world's mineral wealth are we entitled in preserving our comfortable manner of living? How much to save our skins? Can survival be bought at too great a cost to others? Are we free to mortgage the future? Was it Stuart Chase who, a quarter century ago, rephrased the Golden Rule to read, "Do both to the born and the unborn as you would have them do unto you?"

"Poverty, Powerlessness, The Church," W. Astor Kirk, *Concern*, 1965

Editor's Note: Kirk explores whether or how churches will participate in the national war on poverty program that was part of the Economic Opportunity Act of 1964 and calls on churches to help.

From the article; Will the churches continue to support the poverty war when it becomes apparent that a formerly powerless social group is wielding its new power in its own way?

A widely held viewpoint associated with the national war on poverty program is that churches not only can but will make a significant contribution to that effort.

Outside as well as within the churches this viewpoint seems to be accepted uncritically.

The purpose of this article is to raise some questions, with the hope of stimulating critical examination of the basic assumption that churches will make a fundamental contribution to the effort to eliminate poverty in this country.

I

One important point does not seem to be fully understood by churches. That point is that *poverty* and *powerlessness* go hand in hand. Over long periods of time, powerlessness invariably leads to poverty. But poverty itself is basically a concrete manifestation of powerlessness.

Therefore it is futile to think that a really significant attack on poverty can be made anywhere apart from an effective attack on powerlessness.

In every American community, the poor people are also the individuals and groups who have little or no share in the social power of the community. They are powerless. So long as they remain powerless, it simply will not be possible for them to overcome poverty.

Although it is a matter of common knowledge among students of human society, this plainly evident social fact seems not to be recognized or appreciated by the churches.

To be powerless is to be unable to effectively participate in shaping the social policies of the community, private as well as public. It is a lack of capacity to produce "intended effects" with respect to the behavior of others. Without social power one does not have the ability to make one's interests coin in the decision-making processes of the community.

It is evident that any group of people is without power if it does not possess the capacity to effectively *influence, determine,* or *control* the social policies of the community. The social policies of the community consist of the decision and action whereby community resources and values are authoritatively allocated.

Powerlessness, therefore, is that unhappy status of being unable effectively to participate in the processes that result in authoritative allocation of community resources and values.

This is precisely the status of the poor who live in the midst of plenty— the economically disadvantaged, the socially under-privileged, the culturally deprived, the emotionally distraught, the spiritually bereft.

II

To assume that the churches will contribute significantly to the elimination of poverty is to assume that, in the communities in which they are located, churches will be both disposed and able to help the *powerless* to become *powerful*.

That this assumption is warranted by the known facts about the churches, as social organization, is open to serious question.

One may appropriately ask, first, whether churches can overcome their deeply-rooted bias against talking, thinking, planning, and acting in terms of power concepts.

Church bias against consideration of power concepts is not difficult to understand. The idea that power *per se* is evil is still a strong element in the social mythology of most churches.

Will it be possible in the future for more church leaders, and the rank-and-file church members, to appreciate the fact that responsible exercise of broadly-based social power will be necessary to attain that degree of social justice that will eliminate poverty in their communities?

Apropos is the reminder of Philipp Maur, in his *Politics and Evangelism*, that "We live in a time when there seem to be no remedies for suffering whose origin is political, except political ones."

There is a second area in which questions may be properly raised regarding the probability of effective church action in the war on poverty. Can churches counteract the latent hostility to any fundamental adjustment in existing social arrangement—the structures of power—by which power in the community is shaped and shared?

In every community there are structures of power: institutionalized *patterns* of relationships in accordance with which statutes are determined, roles are assigned, and authority to make decisions on behalf of the community is acknowledged.

These institutionalized patterns constitute what we may call the "power order," i.e., distribution of social power in the community.

The existence of chronic poverty in a community means that social power is so distributed that the "poverty group" is relatively powerless. The complex patterns of relationships are such that this group does not have the capacity effectively to influence, determine, or control the allocation of community resources and values.

In any community churches, at least the dominant ones, have a vested interest in the existing power order. This means that they have a vested interest in a residue of powerlessness.

It remains to be demonstrated that churches can be expected to support willingly the war on poverty on the crucial battleground of that war. The battleground is the point at which decisive action must be taken to *redistribute* social power in the community.

Though they may do so less overtly than other groups that have a stake in the power order, the more powerful Protestant, Catholic, and Jewish congregations will probably resist those radical changes in the social structures of the community that are necessary to provide escalators by which the "poverty group" may join the ranks of the powerful.

An indication that church resistance to such changes may be expected is to be found in Chicago. For Chicago's more prestigious religious leaders have opposed The Woodlawn Organization project sponsored by Saul Alinsky's Industrial Areas Foundation. It is the aim of the project to provide the means by which otherwise powerless groups may become effective participants in the complex process of decision-making in Chicago.

The probability of church resistance to a radical war on poverty program is also indicated in other cities by the opposition to "bussing school children." Some of the most effective opposition has come from churches whose parishioners long ago abandoned the ideas (and institution) of the corner grocery store, but who still cling tenaciously to the myth of the "neighborhood school."

The war on poverty will not be a success in any community unless the social strategists planning the war can devise some way to build a more secure base of social power among the powerless. At this juncture in that war effort, despite all the hullabaloo about "the Christian case against poverty," the signs are not too evident that churches will be of much real help to the social strategists.

III

It is possible to identify without difficulty a third area regarding which there may be reasonable doubt that churches will make a fundamental contribution to the war on poverty. Perhaps that area can best be indicated by asking the following question:

Will it be possible for the churches to stop responding traditionally to the rationalization built up to justify and support order under which the powerless—the "poverty groups" in the community—can never become part of the powerful?

In every community there is a vast amount of rationalization in accordance with which existing patterns of distribution are legitimized. These rationalizations make community social structures seem reasonable. They promote the ideas that the fault lies entirely in the powerless group itself and not at all in the system of community relationships that relegates the group to social impotence.

Thus one finds current in every community the standard myths about the poor: they are deficient in character; they have a congenital lack of motivation; they are lazy, thriftless, and happy with their lot.

Unfortunately, there are far too many present indications that churches are among the chief propagators of these myths. In so doing, they help to sustain social patterns that produce and nourish poverty.

The behavior of "human-beings," unlike that of lower animals, is not primarily a product of in-born genetic factors. The fact that the poor lack the cultural values of the middle-class church members cannot be attributed to a demon somewhere locked up inside the poor. The outlook of the poor, their lack of a "fruitful conception of the conscious movement through time toward desired goals," indeed their whole style of life is an inevitable product of the "culture" of powerlessness.

Dan W. Donson rightly observes that "it is perhaps impossible for a youth who is a member of a group that is powerless in a community to grow to maturity without some trauma to the perception of himself because of the compromised position of his group." Churches that fail to recognize or act in accordance with this basic fact cannot make a fundamental contribution to the war on poverty.

Responding traditionally to the rationalizations of the powerful, churches seek to express their "religious" concern for the powerless through some form of activity commonly called "service." It is a strange paradox that what the churches do under the rubric of service, and the manner in which they do it, often contribute to the destruction of the little self-esteem that the poor have.

In the final analysis service rendered to and for the powerless by the powerful, compromises the powerless in the integrity of their selfhood. Moreover, all too often such service develops distorted perceptions of the inherent superiority on the part of the powerful.

Engaging in service activities under church auspices may provide middle-class church members with the opportunity they need "to buy a clear conscience." It is much easier for the powerful to render services to the poor than it is for them to share their power with the poor.

The provision of traditional welfare services, no matter how important they may be, does not get at the root of the problem of the "poverty group." The root of the problem is powerlessness. Unless large expenditures of public funds are involved, the provision of welfare services usually does not arouse the suspicion of the power order of the community. On the other hand, such suspension and hostility do occur where efforts are made to develop aggressive leadership among the poor for an attack on community social policies sanctioned by the power order.

This is well-illustrated by the experience of the Mobilization for Youth (MFY) in the Lower East Side of New York City. MFY's community development programs have come under severe criticism from the political power structure, and from the leadership of the Lower East Side's "private establishment," MFY's sponsorship of rent strikes, its encouragement of civil right groups, and its work with parent groups that supported the school boycott have drawn sharp protest from the powerful.

Another target of the critics has been the Legal Services Unit established by the MFY. Through this community action project counsel is provided for low-income and minority-group members whose rights might be threatened by the exercise of public authority in such programs as welfare, public housing, unemployment insurance, and the administration of criminal law.

Thus when the MFY's activities began to go beyond "squirting a little more welfare" on the poor, when the poor on the Lower East Side were encouraged to organize and shake off their apathy, the power order of the community opposed those activities. All of the rationalizations built up to support the existing structures were employed effectively by the opponents of the MFY's activities. All sorts of accusations were made. A city-sponsored investigation was conducted and revealed that there was little substance to the charges. But the investigators recommended that MFY discontinue its social action programs!

Title II of the war on poverty act (Economic Opportunity Act of 1964) authorizes federal support of community action programs in local communities. The declared purposes of these programs are to encourage and assist communities "to mobilize their resources to combat poverty through community action programs."

The most significant contribution that churches could make on this battle front of the war against poverty is to insure that in each community where there is a Title II program supported by federal funds, one of its objectives shall be to assist the poor in acquiring the social power necessary to help themselves.

IV

Finally, the assumption that churches will contribute significantly to the elimination of poverty is based on the premise that churches will really come to understand a fundamental fact of human society, which may be stated as follows: Social power is never freely bestowed upon a powerless group by the powerful, but has to be acquired by the powerless group through its confrontation of and encounter with the powerful.

It is a central thesis of this article that "poverty groups" in most American communities are relatively powerless. They do not possess the capacity to insure the actualization of their purposes or the protection of their interests through established communal decision-making processes.

In the final analysis, the dimension of poverty that is rooted in powerlessness can only be dealt with effectively by changing those patterns of community relationships that relegate groups of people to social impotence. The status-influence structures of congregations in affluent neighborhoods being what they are; it may be too optimistic to assume that churches can help the poor achieve a significant encounter with the powerful.

There are two implications of this viewpoint that need to be stressed. In the first place the challenge facing churches is to recognize that groups who have social power and advantage are usually complacent with respect to the situation of the poor. They do not, as a rule, change either attitudes or their behavior in the communal decision-making councils unless pressure is put on them by those whose interests would be served by a change of conditions. Persuasion is seldom an adequate lever. Socially, politically, and economically privileged groups do not even see the facts that characterize the lot of the underprivileged until they are forced to look at them.

Secondly, churches must come to realize that powerless groups in the community can hardly expect to achieve an effective encounter with the powerful if the ground rules governing the confrontation are determined solely by the powerful themselves. Those who have deployed boycotts, sit-ins, and marches, on principle, as being outside the communally established rules of protest and pressure, simply have not understood this basic fact. There is a combination of pressure and persuasion when a local merchant in a low-income neighborhood discovers that he has lost 95 per cent of his customers because of his discriminator employment policies. In northern cities, rebellion against slums, schools that do not educate, and unemployment also have the dual character of persuasion and pressure.

The ground rules set by the powerful order of the community makes it possible for the powerful to exercise covert and hence concealed pressure on the powerless. Those with power may discharge employees; they may evict tenants; or they may refrain from taking any positive remedial action by dragging their feet. Protection of the interests of the powerfully by foot-dragging is often the most effective form of exercise of social power.

Behind it may lie control of votes, property, corrupted public officials, and the media of public opinion formation.

To make a significant contribution to the war on poverty, churches must be willing to bring essential resources into the confrontation of the powerful by the powerless. They must be disposed to promote organization of "poverty groups" in our communities across the nation. What is needed is organization to give dignity and morale so that the poor can help themselves, organization to bring economic pressure on the community, organization to make effective political decisions—in short, organization to help the powerless acquire the capacity effectively to influence, determine, and control the allocation of community resources and values.

The great challenge that the war against poverty poses from the churches is the challenge to commit themselves to the goal of a new society with *something more* than the rhetoric of Christian idealism. That "something more" is nothing less than the will to engage in whatever action is necessary to help the powerless acquire the social power that will enable them to protect their interest, their integrity, and their human dignity in the councils of communal decision-making.

"Let us opt for Ecology rather than Energy," Allan Brockway, *e/sa*, 1975

Editor's Note: The article reflects on the cost of international oil and restrictions on strip-mining of coal during the Ford Administration. It calls for stewardship of natural resources, and even reflects on the UMB's own use of electricity to conduct its work.

In a world society where the only certainty is the assurance of uncertainty, where basic values conflict with basic values, Christian faith would seem to be a hold on reality that is really reality, or at least it would seem so for Christians. Christians know that no matter what happens, God rules the world. And there's some comfort in that.

But Christians also know that God hasn't interfered directly in the affairs of peoples and nations for a very long time. Moses heard directly from God about the liberation of the Children of Israel. Who has heard the voice from the burning bush concerning the supply of oil or the destruction of oceans or the world-wide recession? We may be forgiven for crying out that God has deserted his human creation.

Christians, though, know something else. They know that they (that is, humanity) have been given the earth and the society to manage, as an apartment building is given into the management of another by its owner. The owner lets the manager know what is expected—and then "goes on a long journey." All problems that arise are the responsibilities of the manager.

We humans manage the earth and the societies that live upon it. The fact that God owns the whole thing does not relieve us of our responsibility. And there's not much comfort in that, if by comfort we mean unambiguous direction about the details of the job.

The details—there's the rub. For a whole host of details have begun to converge and form one massive problem, the solution to what escapes us all: an ever-increasing world population consumes an ever-increasing amount of the limited resources of the earth. How is it possible for all of us to continue living when the earth cannot support us for very much longer in our accustomed manner?

So the details, the specific parts of the massive problem, return to haunt us. Simply because no human mind can comprehend the holistic problem, we focus on representative parts of it. One of the parts is the conflict between the generally acknowledged value of ecological preservation and the need for energy resources. Both are necessary for human survival on earth. But sometimes if we have one we can't have the other—or so it would seem.

On May 20, 1975, President Ford vetoed a bill that would have required reclamation of strip-mined land and would have placed restrictions that such a measure would damage the economy of the United States and its long-term energy capability in addition to harming the economy generally and increasing unemployment. The validity of his reasoning has been, of course, called into question by many inside and outside of Congress, thereby demonstrating the complexity of the energy-ecology problem.

Soon thereafter the President castigated the Congress for inaction of the energy problem and activated his own limited program by adding an additional $1 per barrel to the cost of imported crude oil and took steps to deregulate the price of domestic "old" oil. Speakers for the administration asserted that the President's veto of the strip-mining bill was the most important energy-related action the President had yet taken.

By the strip-mining veto plus the action to increase the price of petroleum products, the President focused attention on the massive problem. President Lyndon Johnson told us that we the American people could have both guns and butter. We the people believed him and the consequences of that belief are now evident in the plight of the US economy. President Ford is telling us that we cannot have both coal and pure rivers, forests, and grazing lands. We tend to believe him, a belief that could well produce unfortunate results in excess of those produced by our belief in "guns and butter."

Proponents of the strip mining bill argued that, far from decreasing coal production, translation of the bill into law cited figures indicating negligible loss for the present and none in the future. On the other hand, should strip mining continue without federal regulation (recognizing that state regulation has begun to rectify some of the more glaring land devastation), more hillsides will be denuded, more chemical run-off will pollute more rivers, and more grazing and farm land will be lost forever. It just may be that, whereas we could not, in actuality, have both guns and butter, we can indeed have both coal and undamaged (or at least reclaimed) land and water.

But let us suppose that we must make a choice. The absolute necessity for energy came home as this Reflections was being written: the lights went out. With the lights went the power to run the antique electric typewriter used to produce Reflections month in and month out. The power did not return for hours, but writing could continue by hand. Not so the other electric-powered machines in the office. The composer that sets the type could not be run by a crank, the light table required for page layouts was useless.

As the editorial staff sat and talked in the silent (no clanking machines) dark, we began to extrapolate on the consequences of weeks and months, not to mention years, of life with no electricity. Most of the artifacts of daily life would no longer be functional, jobs that are now meaningful would vanish into thin air. Human existence in our civilization would change so radically that the change would be intolerable. We must have a continued source of electric energy!

Currently, a large part of our electricity is generated by burning coal. Some is produced by hydroelectric power, some by oil, some by nuclear energy. None is produced by lightning, a "natural" source of electricity. Of all the readily available sources of energy, coal is the most plentiful. Only solar energy is in greater supply and it is, for the near future at least, not readily available. The scales are weighted in favor of energy resources and opposed to ecological resources.

But values, equally important, are inherent in the earth. These are human values (and this Reflections is devoted to human values, not values of the earth per se.) The future of technological society depends on reliable sources of energy but if that energy is derived at the expense of farm and grazing land and pure (or nearly pure) water in creeks and rivers and seas then human life is sustained at one end and diminished at the other. Ultimately the balance scale will shift: energy, such as coal, will be far less important than the earth. But by then it will be too late.

The formula for balancing energy needs against ecological needs escapes us all. But Christians, who know humanity holds the earth and their own societies in trust, can readily recognize that, if the choice between more quick coal and less farm and grazing land, less pure water, less wooded hills, then the choice must be for the latter.

It would be more in keeping with our mandate from God to manage the earth for us to choose to still our electric typewriters rather than make the earth unlivable for generations to come.

But perhaps we don't have to make that radical choice, perhaps there is a middle ground, perhaps the Lord is testing us right now to see whether or not we are competent managers of his "apartment." In that case, we have another chance, probably for a very short time.

While we get on with exploring the "middle ground," let us as a society, burn no bridges behind us. Let us opt for ecology rather than energy. To choose energy is to choose for a future that cannot be reversed. To choose ecology is to leave the options open. And it is to choose that the Lord, the owner of the whole thing, may return to bless us.

"The Poor Are the Hungry," Allan Brockway, *e/sa*, 1977

Editor's Note: This is the introduction from a booklet that GBCS published entitled "Justice in a Hungry World" in response to the quadrennial missional priority of world hunger.

Jesus noted that there will always be poor people when his disciples complained because a woman had anointed him with precious oil instead of selling it and giving the proceeds to a few poor people. The suggestion, of course was that giving some money to a few poor people would do little to solve the problem of poverty, whereas the symbolic purpose for which the oil was used was wholly appropriate. But if anything is clear from the Gospels it is that Jesus was totally committed to the poor. He chose his disciples from among their ranks. He apparently lived in near poverty himself. His acknowledgement that giving alms would not solve the problem is, therefore, even more significant. Today we might say that he knew well the pervasiveness and tenaciousness of social systems.

Jesus had harsh words for the rich. A rich man, he said, could easier squeeze through the eye of a needle then enter the Kingdom of God. If we take that saying at face value, hardly a single one of us Americans has a prayer of reaching God's kingdom (no matter how our theologies define that term). Compared to the rest of the world even the poverty-stricken in the United States are rich. On another occasion, however, Jesus told a story about the servant who cheated his rich master while the master was away on a trip. The censure fell, not on the rich master, but on the servant who had failed to make the master even richer.

It is important to realize that Jesus was not, at least in the passages referred to above, condemning poor or rich individuals. He was instead addressing social systems. The Gospel, the truth that each human being is cosmically loved and held to be valuable, is not conditioned by the number of cars, stocks and bonds, homes, TV sets, farms, and barns an individual may possess. Everyone is eligible for the Kingdom of God.

Those who participate in the rich sector of the social system have a harder time, however, because their participation, in and of itself, makes life intolerable for those in the impoverished sector of the system. Most of us church people live in the rich sector. We have a problem. The problem is not that we are bad or evil people; it is that we are part of a social and economic structure that produces deprivation for others.

We rich people have no alternative but to be involved in our rich social culture. We are who we are. If we sold what we own and gave the proceeds to the poor, the overall problem of poverty would remain unchanged. But if we do not we are condemned. There's nothing like being between the rock and the hard place! But before we begin pitying the poor rich folk (that's us), we need to ask what we can do within the system to change it.

The poor are the hungry. Anywhere in the world food in ample quantity is available to those who have money to buy it. In the United States, it is the aged, the sick, the unemployed, and children who are hungry. Nevertheless, famine has stalked portions of Asia and Africa in recent years and it threatens at any time to become widespread. The world is at the mercy, for instance, of the weather and the climate. Severe and sustained drought in the grain-producing regions of the United States and Canada could quickly produce a world-wide devastating shortage of food.

That need not be, drought or no drought, if we in the rich nations act through our governments to establish food reserves, to encourage appropriate agricultural production in the tropics, create economically viable systems for equitably distributing available food to everyone who needs it, and similar mechanisms. These things can only be done by governments, but only the religious communities can provide the moral bases for government action.

187

During September 1976, the US Senate and House of Representatives adopted similar "Right to Food Resolutions." Both state that "it is the sense of the Congress that the United States affirms the right of every person in this country and throughout the world to food and a nutritionally adequate diet." Churches, church groups, and individual Christians were influential in securing the passage of these resolutions that for the first time establish food as a *right* in US public policy.

A moral foundation for US food policy has been laid. But it will mean nothing unless morally grounded specific actions are taken by the Congress (and the various state legislatures) and are morally implemented by the executive branches of government. And that is where sustained action by churches and church groups becomes crucial.

"The UFW Organizer," George Ogle, *Christian Social Action*, 1988

Editor's Note: The article illustrates in stark, dramatic form the exploitation of migrant workers in food systems. From the article: This is the first in a series of six human interest articles depicting the lives and experiences of California farmworkers. George Ogle, director of the Department of Social and Economic Justice of the General Board of Church and Society, generated this series out of recent contacts with a number of California farmworkers struggling to achieve self-determination through self-organization. Subsequent articles will be written by a farmworker and by others whose work has brought insights into the inequities and injustices unique to this group of US laborers.

"Your father called again, Joe. You better talk to him."

"Yeah, I will. But it doesn't make any difference. He always hounds me on the same thing."

"He wants you to quit the union?"

"Wants me to get a 'real job,' he says, 'You gotta look out for yourself,' he says. 'Unions are a bunch of crap,' he says."

"Food's ready. Let's eat!" Maria Gomez finished putting the evening meal on the table. She and her husband, Joe, an organizer for the United

Farm Workers union (UFW), lived in a small two-bedroom trailer house, not far from Delano. As Maria began to say grace, the phone rang. Even before answering, Joe knew it was Arturo, the union's regional director, and he knew he would not like what Arturo had to say.

"Joe, you've got to pull them out. There is no other way. Milliken is going to shut us out as soon as the contract expires. They've already got the armed guards in place. The only hope is to beat them to the punch."

"I know. I know. We've gone over that," lamented Joe. "But our people aren't ready. I may not be able to get them to pull together. A lot of them are new in the union."

"So what's your alternative?" exploded Arturo. "You know damn well that the company has signed with the Teamsters. They only way to head them off is to stop work. Now!"

"OK! OK! I'll do what I can!" He hung up. He didn't like it at all. Joe Gomez had been a union organizer for only a few years, but it seemed like he had been organizing one thing or another for most of his 35 years. He had organized a soft ball league at age 12, and at 17 had led a sit-in at the city hall on behalf of kids who wanted a summer recreation program.

Joe had gone through college on a football scholarship, and afterwards had become a teacher and coach at a local high school. He thought he had found his calling until a friend introduced him to Cesar Chavez and the United Farm Workers. Within the year he joined the UFW as an organizer in California's vineyards.

Maria's prayer remained unsaid. Joe got up from the table, grabbed his jacket and headed for the door. Maria, who had worked as a farmhand on a ranch that Joe had organized, was disturbed. A phone call at suppertime and Joe running out the door without eating was nothing new. "I'll be back," Joe said as the door slammed shut. Maria sat down and ate.

As Joe hurried through the town, he thought about the people he was going to call upon to strike. Juan was a strong one; Joe could depend on him, but he also had seven children. Lydia was old; her bent back spoke of her 30 years in the fields. Jose and Gloria, husband and wife, always worked together; charter members of the union, their four kids were now in school. Then there were the newcomers—people who were in the fields for the first time—and also a lot of young guys who had come across the border illegally to earn money to take back to Mexico.

Hardworking People

They were all good, hard-working people. To earn their $5.50 an hour, they positioned themselves under the vines, cut the bunch of grapes, caught it and placed it on a tray—all in one quick motion that had to be repeated hundreds of times during the day. After a few hours, even the seasoned cutters were filthy with dirt, bugs and pesticide residues. Pain ricocheted up and down their backs into their shoulders.

Joe struggled with the nagging question of whether or not they could all stick together. The union had won wage increases, health care and better conditions in the field, but now the owners were determined to reverse the gains. A strike could end up with the union people being fired and even blackmailed. Joe knew the fear of losing one's job gnawed away in everyone's gut.

After knocking, Joe walked into the little concrete block house where Andres Gomez, chair of the union's field committee on the Milliken Ranch, lived. The other six members were already there. Including Andres, four were long-time union members; three had joined only in the last year.

Joe reported Arturo's call and explained the situation: the first contract with Milliken had come as a result of the boycott of 1970. Milliken, however, had accepted the union as something forced upon him; he seemed humiliated for having to sign a contract with Cesar Chavez and the UFW. Now he was hitting back.

"Sweetheart" Contract

The contract with the UFW would expire in two days, and then Arthur Milliken intended to sign a "sweetheart" contract with the Teamsters and refuse any further relations with the UFW. The only option left to the union was to seize the initiative—get out on strike tomorrow, expose Milliken's plot, and pray that there would be enough legal and public support to make Milliken and the Teamsters back off.

That night few of the UFW people slept. All night long Joe and the committee members moved from house to house to explain the tactics for the next day: "Follow the lead of the committee. No rough stuff. One false move and the whole sheriff's department will be on our tails."

Morning arrived pink and blue. The workers, however, scarcely noticed the beauty of the day. Apprehension and fear commanded their minds as they began the day's toil. They carried their secret as though guilty of a conspiracy. Quickly they cut the grapes from the vines, but, as instructed by the committee, they left them unpacked.

Milliken's foremen were experiencing their own guilt. They knew that the boss was going to lock the workers out and bring in the Teamsters. That meant trouble, probably violence. Their efforts to conceal their foreknowledge was not convincing. Both foremen and workers acted out their parts.

Slowly the workday came to a close. As Joe appeared at the main road leading into the ranch, the committee members gave the signal. Without hesitation the workers stopped what they were doing and walked out of the fields toward the road.

There they unfurled UFW banners. Garcia organized the workers into picket lines and led them in shouting slogans.

"We are the UFW!"
"Milliken bargain with the UFW!"
"Teamsters do not represent the workers!"
"Long live justice; long live the UFW!"
Above all the noise, Joe shouted:

"Brothers and sisters, we must stick together. The union is our only security. Milliken wants to cut wages, take away the health plan and sell our contract to the Teamsters.

"We have to stay together. No one works until we all work! We're doing this for our families, our own dignity and justice. We will be attacked. Some of us may go hungry. But let us do no violence. Let us stay together.

You will be shown what to do. I hope to meet with Milliken soon to get a new contract."

As Joe spoke, Milliken's security guards came running up the lane, guns ready. Simultaneously the sheriff's cars screeched to a stop on the highway next to where the workers marched. The workers shouted louder, but the sight of the guns sparked feelings of fear.

Joe met Milliken's men as they reached the highway. "Tell Mister Milliken I will be in to see him tomorrow. We'll need to get things settled before those unpacked grapes go bad."

Night had come; the UFW workers had acted; everyone had stuck together. As though reluctantly, they slowly disbursed and drifted homeward. However, Joe and the seven committee members had no thoughts of sleep. They had to set up a schedule for picketing, agree on strategies for negotiations, devise tactics for defending against the Teamsters, and, above all, work to keep everything non-violent.

Bringing in Scabs

Near dawn the next day Joe left the last worker's house and headed home. As he crossed Main Street, he heard trucks. Three of them passed before he realized what was happening: They were bringing in scabs. "The bastards! Scabs!"

Joe ran back to the main entrance of the ranch. Others were already there. The sheriff had known all along. His troops were keeping the highway clear while Milliken's armed guards guided the trucks down the lane. The workers stood by; scabs were taking their jobs.

The fear, only a faint creeping sensation in the back yesterday, now tightly gripped their hearts—*their jobs!* How would they live? Where would they get food for the children? Their fear erupted into shouts and curses. One young man pushed a security guard and was immediately knocked down and thrown in the sheriff's car.

The chief security officer came up to Joe and snarled: "I have a message for you from Mr. Milliken—'Get the hell off my property! If I see you or any of your so-called union people on my land again, I'll have the lot of you thrown in jail.'"

"Get outta here, man" Joe responded. "We'll picket this place until Milliken begs us for a contract."

Joe turned towards his people: "OK, let's picket. Hold the banners up high. Don't block the road. No rough stuff. We'll talk to those scabs after work. Andres, you're in charge. I've got to go report to the union."

For a few days everyone lived on outrage. The workers went to the ranch, shouted union slogans, insulted the scab labor and swore solidarity to each other and the union. But fear grew stronger—they had no job, no food, Milliken refused any compromise. Outrage gave way to necessity. Quietly, hat in hand, head bowed, some went back to Milliken. Others searched up and down the valley for something—anything. The names of the committee members, it was rumored, were circulated by Milliken to other ranches to warn them against hiring such pro-union people.

Maria put the evening meal on the table. Her prayer was not interrupted by Arturo. As they ate, Joe thought out loud: "I can just see my old man now. Probably giving me the sign and saying, 'You stupid jerk. What'd I tell you. Union stuff is crap.' He's probably saying that, isn't he?"

"You know him better than I do."

"But he's wrong! People can't take care of themselves when those rich bastards won't allow them. How can you take care of yourself if you're forced to bow and scrape and be a slave? It's not right—regardless of what my old man says!"

"Joe," Maria asked, "did you hear the news from the Bailey Ranch? Bailey brought in scabs, like down here—but a lot them were former union people, not young kids just brought in from Mexico. The union persuaded Bailey's scabs not to work. It bought them bus tickets to go on to other jobs, and they left.

"Milliken beat us this time, but I think the union has started something bigger than Milliken or Bailey. People are waking up."

The next evening Joe Gomez met Roberto Rodriguez in a local tavern. Roberto was a young man, undocumented from Mexico, whose first job in the United States was at Milliken's ranch. He had ridden into town on the first truck that night; now after several weeks of work, he wanted to hear about the union.

Over a few drinks and a sandwich, Joe Gomez and Roberto Rodriguez began to make plans for an organizing campaign on the Milliken Ranch. As Maria said, the union movement was bigger than Milliken. People were beginning to move.

"Every Child Has the Right to Smile," Shanta M. Bryant, *Christian Social Action*, 1998

Editor's Note: Issues of child labor were taken up by Church and Society alongside Methodist leaders, 2and became a global effort to curb exploitation of children.

Underneath Mohan's right eye lie two scars, visible reminders of his former life as a child laborer in an Indian carpet factory. Although he looks about 10 years old, he's actually 14. When Mohan was six, an employment broker arrived at his village in Saharsa, Bihar, bearing promises to his parents of fair wages, an education, food and housing, for their child's labor. Believing that the arrangement would be in the best interest of their son, Mohan's parents relented.

For three years he and other children from the village slaved in the carpet factory for their "master," as the factory owners are called. Instead of receiving all the promises, the children worked up to 16 hour days, with little food, no education, and regular beatings.

"For the first days I was treated well," said Mohan through a Hindi translation. "They gave me good food." That soon ended, the young boy recalled.

While using sharp, dangerous needles to weave carpets, Mohan accidently cut his face. The "master" shouted, scolded him for allowing himself to be hurt, and warned him not to cry or he would face being hung upside down in a tree by the legs. The young boy's cuts were then treated with salt water.

Mohan is a dreamer with clear bright eyes, lots of energy and an effervescent personality. A curious child, he's always getting into something.

If you take your eyes off of him for two seconds, he's dashing off to something else. One wonders if Mohan is trying to make up for all those years of a missed childhood toiling in the carpet factory producing high-priced carpets that eventually are sold to the United States and throughout the world. "Children shouldn't be working," he testified. "They should have lives as kids."

Freed from the hazardous working conditions in the carpet factory by a raid of the South Asian Servitude Coalition, an Indian non-governmental organization against child labor, he now attends a rehabilitation school and is receiving vocational training.

. . .

An international alliance of more than 1,000 religious, labor, child, and human rights organizations participated. The United Methodist General Board of Church and Society and the General Board of Global Ministries' Women's Division cosponsored the global march. United Methodist churches and related community centers organized forums and provided housing and food to the marchers throughout the US portion.

Thousands turned out in cities around the world to join in the global effort. Core marchers—who had committed at least two weeks—linked with marchers who participated in other regions of the world. Former child laborers attested to their personal struggles working as children while child advocates called for the strengthening of laws to eradicate child labor.

. . .

Poverty often compels parents to send their children off to work in the factories, in homes, on the farms, and on the streets. Low wages and high unemployment may leave poor people with few options, other than committing their children to work to help meet their family's basic needs.

Kailash Satyarthi of India, chair of Global March Against Child Labor, who first conceptualized a march across the world against child labor, emphasized that children should not be blamed for poverty. Instead, he said, the finger should be pointed at nation-states, the global economy and international financial organizations whose policies contribute to a nation's impoverished circumstances.

"Who is responsible for poverty?" said Satyardhi, founder of the South Asia Coalition on Child Servitude that has liberated some 28,000 children from bonded labor. "It's not the responsibility of the child. It's the World Bank and International Monetary Fund, not the poor children. Why the hell do they have to be responsible for it?"

Countries using child labor justify the practice, saying that due to dire poverty it's necessary and will be tolerated only temporarily until they can compete in the globalized economic system. Ali Taqi, assistant director-general of the ILO, refuted this justification and stressed that child labor, itself, is a cause of poverty. "If children are condemned to hard labor, how will they have the skills to grow and enter the modern economy?" said Taqi, a Pakistani national.

. . .

Since child laborers cannot work and go to school at the same time, the "survival" of the family may take precedence over the children's education.

In the United States, for example, labor laws allow child farm workers to work legally before and after school. Consequently, they may come to school late, miss classes, fall asleep during class and face detention or suspension. The difficulty of managing school and work forces many to drop out. When they are faced with the choice of making money to support the family or pursuing an education, education frequently loses out.

"Money means more than education," said Diane Mull of the child workers who do not complete their schooling. Mull, a core US marcher, serves as executive director of the Virginia-based Association of Farmworker Opportunity Program, a farm worker advocacy and educational organization.

. . .

Representatives of government, businesses, and unions met in Switzerland to discuss a new ILO Convention on Child Labor, in which officials hope to propose new international legal standards for the immediate eradication of extreme forms of child labor.

Emotional Testimonies to World Leaders

For the first time in the history of the ILO meeting, more than 300 former child workers from four continents marched into the UN Assembly Hall to give emotional testimonies of their lives before world leaders. As the children marched in, delegates gave them a standing ovation.

The new standards call for an abolition of the extreme forms of child labor, including:

- slavery and slavery-like practices;

- forced labor, debt bondage and serfdom;

- use of children in illegal activities, prostitution and pornography;

- any work or activity that will jeopardize the health, safety or morals of children.

US Labor Secretary Herman, who headed the US delegation to the ILO meeting, said that President Bill Clinton is committed to the agenda to combat child labor—internationally and at home. "We need to do more to put it on the global agenda," Herman said recently. "We are actively looking at solutions to end child labor."

However, US child advocates are pressing for their government to live up to its word and ratify the new international standards on child labor and the Convention on the Rights of the Child (CRC). The 1973 convention on abolishing child labor was ratified by about 60 countries.

The United States is the only organized world government that has not ratified the CRC, which includes provisions on eliminating child labor. Somalia, which does not have a government, is the only other country that has not signed the convention.

Pharis Harvey, a United Methodist clergyman, who sat on the march's International Steering Committee, said it was an "embarrassment" to explain why the United States has not ratified the CRC. "I'm sorry to say that the government doesn't think it's important enough," he lamented.

With the success of the global effort to raise awareness about child labor, advocates are hoping that government leaders will take action.

"The main reason for child labor is the lack of social consciousness, the lack of political will, and that few laws are enforced," 13-year-old Asmita, a child advocate and daughter of global march organizer Satyarthi, said forcefully. The Indian teen called on all governments to act immediately to eliminate child labor worldwide. "Every child has the right to smile and to be a child," she asserted.

"When the 'Promised Land' Garbage Dump Collapsed," Mervin Toquero, *Christian Social Action*, 2000

Editor's Note: This article shows the intersections of poverty, globalization, and environmental crises in marginalized communities in the Philippines.

From the article: Mervin Toquero was the coordinator of Environmental Concerns, the National Council of Churches in the Philippines. CSA thanks Levi Bautista for his help in securing this article.

Payatas. In the Philippines, the name evokes an image of extreme poverty, a place where a mountain of filth dominates the landscape, a place where houses sit precariously in heaps and bounds of garbage. It's a place where people eke out their living in smelly and dirty surroundings, where the country's poorest of the poor reside, where people who have been pushed to the margins of society have converged to build their future from the refuse of society.

Payatas. Some people call it "Lupang Pangako" or "the Promised Land." Day after day, monstrous trucks unload tons of waste from millions of people in the surrounding metropolis of Manila; waste that is their livelihood. It is a promised land for people who have nowhere left to go.

Payatas. On July 10, 2000, the Philippine's symbol of extreme poverty, the mountain of garbage, collapsed, killing more than 200 people. Many more were wounded, many still are missing, and more than 200 families have lost their homes. People who live off garbage were killed by garbage.

The Philippines, like the biblical Promised Land, is a land teeming with milk and honey, rich in natural resources, from its minerals to its fertile lands and productive waters. Payatas has become not only a symbol of extreme poverty but the embodiment of economic injustice, political insensitivity, and spiritual void.

Microcosm of the Country

The Payatas dump is three times the size of a football field. The shantytown is home to at least 60,000 people, some who have been there for all of the dump's 27 years of operation. The dump absorbs a quarter of the 4,500 metric tons of solid waste churned out daily by factories and homes within metropolitan Manila, home to 10 million people.

The economic activity in the area is a complex system. The trucks that bring the refuse to Payatas are controlled by local government officials who profit from the operation. The junk shops where the shantytown dwellers sell the things they've collected also pay their "rents" to local officials. The junk shops sell the "semi-processed garbage" to middlemen who in turn sell it to factories. The big profits from the filth go to those who are already rich and powerful, while the people of Payatas merely eke out their existence.

To say that Payatas is a microcosm of Philippine society would be a very apt description. The Philippines, home to 75 million people, is a "dumping ground" for surplus products and a haven for capital of many First World countries. This "process" of dumping surplus goods and exploitative capital from foreign monopoly capitalists is facilitated by a few Filipinos who control the country. These few also profit from the business of garbage.

The Philippines also is a source for raw materials for many big multi-national and trans-national companies. This leaves the Philippines with depleted ecological resources. Some of the places that bear the ravages of extraction from the mining process have become virtual wastelands.

Economic Troubles

To further the problem, since Joseph Ejercito Estrada (known by the nickname Erap) became the 13th President of the Republic of the Philippines, the price of oil and other petroleum products has increased 12 times. All this despite the Philippine peso's (Php) 18.6 billion "retained earnings" of the big three oil companies: Shell, Caltex, and Petron. The increase in the price of oil will most certainly affect the price of basic commodities.

The inflation rate in the Philippines is at a relatively low 5 to 5.5 percent. According to the IBON Foundation, a local think-tank, the low inflation rate "in the fundamentally weak economy only confirms weak consumer demand and slow importation (IBON Economic and Political Briefing)." The present daily minimum wage is less than half of what is needed for an average family of four to live decently.

More than 4 million Filipinos have no job, with 1.6 million jobs lost in agriculture alone, and another 160,000 in industry. As of May, 600,000 workers were laid off due to closures and retrenchments of many industries. Thousands of farmers and peasants were also economically (and literally) displaced due to the cancellation of Emancipation Patents (EP) and Certificates of Land Ownership (CLOA). In Mindanao alone, 300,000 farmers were dislocated because of the cancellations. These Eps and CLOAs were granted farmers during the land reform program of a previous administration. "Development projects" were the reasons given for the cancellations and the eventual land conversions.

The Philippine's foreign debt is at $52.4 billion as of March 2000, which is an increase of over 4.5 billion since Estrada came to power. The peso continues to weaken. The government continues to borrow money, in part to finance an all-out war in Mindanao. The deficit is also caused by short-falls due to numerous tax holidays granted to big foreign and local corporations and trade liberalizations. The latter was to blame for the influx of cheap foreign products, which has clobbered the local business and agricultural sector.

Further Aggravations

The above problems will be further aggravated, and possibly send even more people to Payatas, by the food security policy of the Estrada administration, which relies on food imports to supply the country's food. This year alone, the Philippines has imported 1.35 million metric tons of rice, up from 0.16 metric tons just six years ago. The proliferation of cheap imported goods, like chicken and beef from the United States and Australia, pose dangers to the health of Filipinos, as food must be shipped great distances to reach their shores.

To reduce government spending and to encourage investors, the government has privatized services that previously were the sole responsibility of government. Many public hospitals, state colleges and universities, the national water system and other services have been transferred to the management of private corporations. The price of these basic services has since gone up, becoming too exorbitant for the regular person.

While millions of Filipinos are reeling from this crisis, rampant graft and corruption prevail. A World Bank report cites that Php 2 billion has been lost due to graft and corruption since 1998. Marcos cronies have continued to receive special favors from the Estrada government. What the cronies did for the economy is to further isolate other business and foreign investors, just to satisfy their kleptocracy.

Living in Poverty

The people of Payatas are consigned to outcasts of society. The "Promised Land" has not benefited from the president's campaign promise of "Erap par sa Mahirap" (Erap for the Poor). The people of Payatas have access to electricity and water, not because of the assistance from the government but from their own initiatives. The people's organizations themselves have put up day care, learning centers, and clinics. Not a single promise to alleviate their sorry condition and to make lives better was fulfilled by Erap. His response to the tragedy was to order the dumps closed, effectively cutting off the means of livelihood for the people.

The rest of the country's poor have also not benefited from Erap's political slogan. Just like his predecessors, Erap has done very little for the 70 percent of the population that lives below the poverty line. According to a 1995 report by the National Census and Statistics Office, three out of five Filipino children live in poverty, one in 20 dies before the age of five, four out of five have no access to early child development programs, and 2.9 million children are laborers (other estimates say as many as 12 million).

Instead of channeling resources to basic services like food, clothing, shelter, health and education, a majority of the nation's budget goes to foreign debt service, the police, and the military. Institutions for basic services have been privatized, often making them inaccessible to the vast majority of people. To make matters worse, the police and military have been called out to quell the growing unrest among the people in their search for a better life.

Foraging Among the Rubbish

During an ecumenical church service of solidarity given for the relatives of the victims of Payatas, Delia Badion, a local leader, shared this message:

"All of us are in mourning and are lamenting the loss of lives of our loved ones due to the tragedy. We acknowledge that all of us live on a mountain of garbage, poor, with no jobs, no decent homes, unschooled, dirty and of foul smell. But I know, and all of us know, how to live in and with dignity.

It is not our fault that we are poor. It is also not our desire to live amidst filth. Who among us would like to live like this, to sacrifice our bodies and our lives in the middle of this deadly sea of garbage in order to keep body and soul together?

Maybe it has not crossed your minds, but we, the poor, have long been suffering from this situation. Due to poverty, maybe some of us believe that it is better for death to come and get us, for maybe death is a better fate than to continue languishing in this hell-like world. Maybe in heaven, there are decent homes and jobs in store for us. Maybe in heaven, education is free.

Every day, while we are reminded of our hapless condition and the frivolous prosperity of the few, myriad questions keep cropping up in our minds and dreams.

We would like to ask these questions of you: What kind of government and society belittles us who are poor? What kind of government is this that looks down on our poverty and glories in the misery of the poor and even scolds us for our intransigence which is to insist to inhabit and live off the garbage? What kind of government is this that has boasted of building 350,000 houses every year, but can't even give free houses to the 34 families who are victims of the landslide in Payatas last year? What kind of government is this that lets the price of basic commodities rise to astronomical levels in the midst of rampant unemployment?

Why are there people who need to forage among rubbish to live? Why is it that there are beggars? Why is there a need for many to shed tears of sorrow while a few gloat and laugh?

Maybe you know the answer to these questions. I hope that everyone can reflect on the true reasons surrounding the tragedy that happened in the Promised Land.

Even birds desire to be free and live abundantly. That is also our wish. May the wounds brought about by tragedy serve as a lesson to all of us."

"COP26 On the Ground: Women and Girls are Leading Climate Solutions," John Hill, *Faith in Action*, 2021

Editor's Note: As part of Church and Society's continued work on climate change, the agency maintained diplomatic relations with the annual global conference to address the environmental crisis. This article highlights how women have increasingly been seen as leaders of the movement.

Tuesday Nov. 9th was gender day at the COP—highlighting both the disproportionate impact climate change has on women and girls and the ways in which women and girls are leading climate solutions in the frontlines of their communities and as policy-makers in elected offices at all levels of government.

Delegates were reminded of the many ways climate change is a matter of gender justice. For example:

- Extreme weather and slow-onset events such as drought and sea-level rise impact the ability of women and girls to secure safe water and food for themselves and their families.

- Each year, an estimated 4 million girls gloebally will be unable to complete their education because of climate-related disruptions.

- Women and girls forced to flee from climate-fueled disasters face a heightened threat of gender-based violence, including forced marriage, rape, and trafficking.

These impacts and so many others highlight just how intertwined climate justice and gender justice are and how imperative it is that any climate solutions are informed by the experiences, voices, and decisions of women. In addition to high-level ministerial presentations from U.S. Speaker of the House Nancy Pelosi and First Minister of Scotland Nicola Sturgeon, gender day elevated voices of women from indigenous communities and young women climate leaders around the world. All of them are helping delegates and observers understand how critical it is to have gender justice at the heart of climate justice.

As speaker after speaker pointed out, for this to happen, women need to be at the table, in the negotiations, shaping the decisions. As Minister Sturgeon observed, when the 120+ world leaders gathered at the start of COP26 precious few were women. Overall at COP26, only 33 percent of all delegates are women.

This needs to change. I am grateful for the strong leadership of women across our Methodist delegation—preaching, teaching, and advocating for climate justice. Comprising 80% of our delegation, women have been the cornerstone of our contributions here at COP26.

In her plenary address Brianna Fruean, a young climate advocate from Samoa, invited us all "to plant seeds of hope that will grow into justice." She then reminded us of the consistent, daily, faithful work necessary for those seeds to grow. I pray that her voice—and the voices of women climate advocates—will reach the ears of and change the hearts of those negotiating the final decision text.

And may they echo and encourage us all long after we have left Glasgow, Scotland, and returned to our daily work of climate justice.

Epilogue / Prologue

Rev. Dr. Susan T. Henry-Crowe

Although his words are often misunderstood as meaning the past predicts the future, Antonio in Shakespeare's *The Tempest* actually says, "Whereof what's past is prologue; what to come in yours and my discharge." With this in mind, we now come to celebrate a century of witness on behalf of Methodist and Evangelical United Brethren churches in the United States of America's seat of government on Capitol Hill. The 1923 vision and intent for the building was for there to be a Methodist presence and faith witness in the heart of this government serving as a beacon, a conscience, and a vision of "our better angels."

This anthology highlights the focus of social witness on Capitol Hill. The issues of health and wholeness, civil and human rights, peace, and economy and ecology have long stood as the cornerstones of this our social witness. Racial justice and equity are the lens we wear.

I write this epilogue/prologue when the world is shattering, and many countries are becoming more authoritarian and nationalistic.

It is not unlike the early twentieth century. In the USA and its territories, this republic and the democratic processes are more fragile and frayed than in prior decades: Evidence for this can be seen in the fact that the 2022 midterm election cycle was held for the first time in 50 years without full protection of the right to vote for minority voters. The Supreme Court has rescinded the rights of women to act in the best interest of themselves, their bodies, and their families. Gun violence is pervasive with little legislative oversight. Russia is invading and occupying parts of Ukraine. Atrocities and horrors of war abound around the globe. Calls for disarmament of nuclear weapons and other weapons of mass destruction are at a fever pitch. Human rights around the world are under attack by governments and states. Health for all, environmental justice, and care of creation are still a far-off vision. Forced migration globally is increasing at a rapid rate. There are movements for the splintering of communities and churches. These are just a few of the challenges we are currently facing.

A review of *The Voice, Methodist Peace Courier, Concern, Engage/Social Action, Christian Social Action, Faith in Action,* and other twentieth-century publications of the General Board of Church and Society and its predecessor bodies demonstrates hauntingly parallel injustices with our current era.

"What's past is prologue" is not about history but rather an invitation of "what to come in your and my discharge." What is the future we will not only envision but help fashion? The cornerstones are laid, the trust is built, the vision is cast, the resources are abundant. In this world that is both radically different and eerily similar, what is our task?

This witness is not linear. It is a journey for justice. It begins by grappling with broken societal ills that are addressed but never completely perfected. It is a journey of walking alongside the most vulnerable and invisible who often are overlooked or cannot speak for themselves—children living in poverty; communities that are hidden away; young people living with mental health issues; aging persons; those living with disabilities. Towns and villages are occupied, destroyed and with no communication systems. Climate that harms rather than paradise that saves. Our Christian faith invites us into this journey toward justice for all. This summons appeals to our resolve as well as our curiosity and hope for a shared future that occupies abundant places and spaces for flourishing and fullness. In this future, children laugh, grasslands are lush, mountains are snow-capped, water is clean, space is magnificent, families live in joy, and death and fear are no more.

This one-hundred-year journey is not epilogue but prologue that belongs to our discharge. We are not bound by our past but set free to clear a path to walk into a more just future. Because of God's vision for a clean, free, healthy, abundantly resourced world we are released from sin and doubt, from fear and death. Our discharge is into a still-broken world on a journey of hope, life, love, and resurrection.

Discussion Questions

1. Read Matthew 25:41-46 and "A Time for the Church to Redefine a Nation" by Rev. Joseph Lowery (p. 118). How do these words from Jesus, according to Rev. Lowery, become a Christian maxim for social action?

2. Read "Johnny Imani Harris: Dignity for Death Row" (p. 103), "We Can't Let It Happen Again!" (p. 110), and "Siege at Wounded Knee" (p. 80). How does each article highlight how racism and colonialism contribute to injustice? What strategies did each case employ to respond to the injustice? Where was the church in these moments and was it effective in responding? Why or why not?

3. Read "Death, Disappearance and Despair" by Miok Fowler (p. 166) and "Journey on the Underground Railroad" with America Sosa (p. 98). Identify the push-pull factors of migration/immigration. Then, read "A New American Immigration Policy" (p. 75). What does this article suggest about the system of immigration in the United States? How has racial/ethnic discrimination informed immigration policy?

4. Read "COP26 on the Ground" (p. 202), "There Is Another World 'Out There'" (p. 39), "A Review of the Continuing Effort to Resolve the Infant Formula Issue" (p. 43), and "Every

Child Has the Right to Smile" (p. 192). How does the lived reality of women and girls in marginalized communities inform advocacy on reproductive justice, civil and human rights, climate, economic justice, and peace?

5. Read "An Exploration of the Problems of a Just and Enduring Peace" (p. 139), "To Follow the Way of Peace" (p. 159), and "The UFW Organizer" (p. 188). Each article discusses the work of solidarity. How does each article illustrate the idea of solidarity? Where else do you see solidarity as critical for Christian social action?

Bibliography

American Library Association. 2019. *Indigenous Tribes of Washington, D.C.* April 17. Accessed August 29, 2022. http://www.ala.org/aboutala/indigenous-tribes-washington-dc.

Anand, Anita. 1982. "A Continuing Effort To Resolve the Infant Formula Issue." *engage/social action*, January: 4-8, 51.

Bagby, Grover C. 1975. "National Health Insurance." *engage/social action*, April: 10-12.

Behney, J. Bruce, and Paul H. Eller. 1979. *The History of the Evangelical United Brethren Church*. Nashville: Abingdon Press.

Board of Christian Social Concerns. 1964. "Population Growth and Human Well-Being." *Concern*, July 15: 7-9.

Board of Church and Society. 1980. "Congress Acts on Iran Crisis: A Call for Reconciliation." *engage/social action*, June: 5-6, 9-15.

—. 1977. "The Poor Are the Hungry." *engage/social action*, April: 18-19.

Board of World Peace. 1958. "Getting Stewardship Out of Knee-Pants!" *Methodist Peace Courier*, April: 1,3.

—. 1957. "The Significance of December 10." *Methodist Peace Courier*, November: 2.

Brockway, Allan R. 1975. "Let Us Opt For Ecology Rather Than Energy." *engage/social action*, July: 2-4.

Bryant, Shanta M. 1998. "'Every Child Has the Right to Smile'." *Christian Social Action*, July/August: 10-14.

Charles F. Boss, Jr. 1939. "The Log."

Corbett, J. Elliott. 1965. "A New American Immigration Policy." Concern, August 1-15: 7-9.

—. 1975. "Handgun Control." *engage/social action*, February: 54-55.

Council of Bishops. 1986. "In Defense of Creation: The Nuclear Crisis and a Just Peace." *Christian Social Action*, June: 8-19.

Council-Austin, Mary. 1986. "We Say NO to Contra Aid!" *engage/social action*, October: 2.

Darling, Dallas. 1991. "To Follow the Way of Peace." *Christian Social Action*, July/August: 34-35.

engage/social action. 1965. "A New Way of Life is Needed." March: 8-9.

Fassett, Thom White Wolf. 1991. "Torn By the Contradictions of War in the Middle East." *Christian Social Action*, February: 4.

Feliciano-Valera, Juan G. 1999. "Practicing 'Misericordia'—'Misery of the Heart.'" *Christian Social Action*, February: 9.

General Commission on Archives and History. n.d. *Heritage Landmarks: A Traveler's Guide to the Most Sacred Places in The United Methodist Church.* Accessed March 16, 2023. http://www.gcah.org/research /travelers-guide.

Gorrell, Donald K. 1988. "A Unique and Pliable Type of Literature: The Social Principles—Eighty Years After the Social Creed." *Christian Social Action*, April: 6.

Harvey, Jane Hull. 1981. "A Pillar of Fire Gave Them Light." *engage/social action*, September: 2-7.

Joiner, J.E. 1953. "The Methodist Building." *The Voice*, November.

Journal of the 1972 General Conference of The United Methodist Church. Commission on The General Conference.

Kelly, Leontine. 1975. "Freedom of Personhood: For All Persons." *engage/ social action*, April: 32-34.

Kirk, W. Astor. 1965. "Poverty, Powerlessness, The Church." *Concern*, May 1: 10-12.

Kuhn, Donald. 1963. "They Came, They Marched, They Departed." *Concern*, September 15: 13-15.

Lowery, Joseph. 2000. "A Time for the Church to Redefine a Nation." *Christian Social Action*, July/August: 4-7.

May, Felton E. 1994. "Alcohol Use and Abuse: A Family Affair." *Christian Social Action*, January: 12-13.

McClean, Robert. 1998. "Standing Up For Human Rights." *Christian Social Action*, December: 4-7.

Ogle, George. 1988. "The UFW Organizer." *Christian Social Action*, April: 18-20.

Oxnam, G. Bromley. 1941. "An Exploration of the Problems of a Just and Enduring Peace." *When Hostilities Cease: Addresses and Findings of the Exploratory Conference on the Bases of a Just and Enduring Peace.* Chicago: Commission on World Peace. 7-14.

Ranck, Lee. 1973. "Siege at Wounded Knee." *engage/social action*, May: 6-21.

Social Principles Study Commission. 1970. "Report of the Social Principles Study Commission." *Journal of the 1970 Special Session of the General Conference of The United Methodist Church.*

Sosa, America. 1986. "Journey on the Underground Railroad." *engage/social action*, January: 26-30.

Stewart, Margy. 1987. "Johnny Imani Harris: Dignity on Death Row." *engage/social action*, September: 4-10.

The Board of Social and Economic Relations of The Methodist Church. 1957. "A Statement on Public School Integration and Law Observance." September.

The Board of Temperance. 1952. "Dr. C.R. Hooton Supports the Johnson-Case Bill, At the Hearings." *The Voice*, January: 10.

The Board of Temperance, Prohibition, and Public Morals of the Methodist Episcopal Church. 1924. "Lynching is Murder." *The Voice*, February: 2.

——. 1930. "Negro leaders for Prohibition." *The Voice*, May: 4.

"The Dedication of The Methodist Building," Clarence True Wilson Collection, Methodist Collection, Drew University, Madison, New Jersey, 1924.

"The Episcopal Address of the Bishops of the Methodist Church to the General Conference 1952." General Conference Proceedings. Nashville: Methodist Publishing House, 181.

Thomas, James S. 1992. *Methodism's Racial Dilemma: The Story of the Central Jurisdiction*. Nashville: Abingdon Press.

Toquero, Mervin. 2000. "When the 'Promised Land' Garbage Dump Collapsed." *Christian Social Action*, September/October: 4-6.

Wilson, Clarence True. 1930. "Twentieth Annual Report of Clarence True Wilson." *The Voice*, January: 1-2, 4, 8.

Printed in the USA
CPSIA information can be obtained
at www.ICGtesting.com
CBHW050719021223
2286CB00005B/9